Becoming a Professor

Becoming a Professor

A Guide to a Career in Higher Education

Marie Iding and R. Murray Thomas

ROWMAN & LITTLEFIELD
Lanham • Boulder • New York • London

Published by Rowman & Littlefield
A wholly owned subsidiary of The Rowman & Littlefield Publishing Group, Inc.
4501 Forbes Boulevard, Suite 200, Lanham, Maryland 20706
www.rowman.com

Unit A, Whitacre Mews, 26-34 Stannary Street, London SE11 4AB

British Library Cataloguing in Publication Information Available

Library of Congress Cataloging-in-Publication Data Available

ISBN 978-1-4758-0915-2 (cloth : alk. paper)
ISBN 978-1-4758-0916-9 (pbk. : alk. paper)
ISBN 978-1-4758-0917-6 (electronic)

♾™ The paper used in this publication meets the minimum requirements of American National Standard for Information Sciences Permanence of Paper for Printed Library Materials, ANSI/NISO Z39.48-1992.

Printed in the United States of America

Contents

Preface

The contents of this book have been drawn from the experiences of two university professors, their colleagues, and their former students who are now professors themselves. The authors' experiences are complemented by their research in educational psychology, in online learning, and in human development.

The book's two authors have between them over sixty years of university teaching experience, supplemented by other teaching and education-related work. Marie Iding, in addition to teaching in California and Hawai'i, has taught numerous courses and workshops elsewhere including American Samoa, Chuuk (formerly Truk, in the Federated States of Micronesia) and Vietnam. She has presented educational psychology research at international conferences in Germany, Australia, Fiji, Switzerland, South Africa, Jamaica, Kenya, Poland, Portugal, Scotland, and Spain, and has published educational research in diverse professional journals. She has lived and conducted studies in Bergen (Norway) and Copenhagen (Denmark).

R. Murray Thomas has lived and taught in Hawai'i, Indonesia, California, Illinois, Washington, and New York. He has also conducted educational research in American Samoa. In addition to teaching, Murray served as the first permanent dean of the school of education at the University of California, Santa Barbara. He is the author, coauthor, or editor of fifty-nine books related to education and human development and has over 350 other professional publications (academic journal and encyclopedia articles, research reports, book chapters, book reviews) to his name. He was the founder and director of the International Education Program at the University of California, Santa Barbara.

Between them, the authors have been teaching continuously since the 1940s. Murray was Marie's professor when she was a graduate student at the University of California, Santa Barbara. Today, they communicate via Skype, a medium that has enabled Murray (from his home in California) to be a guest lecturer for university courses that Marie was teaching in Honolulu.

Both authors truly enjoy working in higher education. They are rewarded by the successes of their current and former students, many of whom keep in touch for years after completing their programs of study and become professors, researchers, and administrators in U.S. institutions and institutions abroad.

Both authors appreciate how the challenges in teaching have forced them to grow as instructors and as individuals. They relish the autonomy they have had in designing courses—selecting readings, planning courses of study, attempting novel instructional techniques. They prefer teaching at the post-secondary level over teaching in elementary or high schools because, in addition to classroom instruction, a major part of their work involves doing research—learning more about the fields that interest them, conducting studies, and writing articles and books. In their professorial role, they have served on and chaired committees responsible for student admissions (deciding which applicants will be accepted as students), for scholarships (deciding which students deserve financial support), for promotions (deciding which colleagues will be advanced to higher levels on the professorial ladder), for selection (hiring new faculty) and more.

Professors and instructors in higher education have a level of autonomy and variety that is typically not available to high school and elementary school teachers, such as what classes they will teach and what instructional methods they will use. Most of their students—and especially those at the graduate level—are enthusiastic scholars, eagerly pursuing challenging learning tasks. And, for the most part, college teachers need not cope with meddling parents.

In sum, a career in higher education can be very rewarding, indeed.

During the writing of this book, we—the authors—incurred a substantial debt of gratitude to our students and colleagues who, over the decades, schooled us in what college and university life can be like from the vantage points of both the receivers and the conveyors of skills and knowledge. To them we offer our thanks. We particularly wish to thank the Faculty Mentoring Program at the University of Hawai'i and the following persons who contributed to the development of case studies, reviewed chapters, or made other contributions: Leonard Davidman, Peter Dill, William Fairbanks, Leonard Garrison, Kris Hanselman, and Jacqui Lipton. We also wish to gratefully acknowledge each other's contributions as authors—Murray's as the primary author of chapters 2, 3, 4, 6, 10, and 12, and Marie's as primary author of chapters 5, 7, 8, 9, and 11.

Marie K. Iding, Honolulu, Hawai'i
R. Murray Thomas, Los Osos, California

ONE

Higher Education's Significant Contexts

The professional life of every faculty member in higher education institutions is pursued in a variety of contexts or environments. All students know about the classroom setting because they directly witness how professors perform there. And when students engage in independent study projects or prepare theses or dissertations, they learn what professors are like in an office environment. But the typical student knows little or nothing about a variety of other contexts that are critical to a faculty member's success, satisfaction, and even survival in academia. The purpose of this book is to solve that problem by describing in detail faculty members' experiences in such environments.

The book has been designed especially for three kinds of readers:

- Graduate students and others who are thinking about launching a teaching career in a higher education institution—in a two-year or four-year college, a university that offers graduate studies, a technical institute, or the like.
- New instructors and professors in higher education institutions who wish to ensure successful careers.
- Individuals who already teach in a post-secondary institution and who wish to rethink and perhaps revise the way they have been doing their job.

It is important to recognize that students and professors have distinctly different perspectives and experiences. Attending lectures is not the same as creating and delivering them. Completing homework assignments differs from planning assignments and evaluating them. Answering test questions involves different skills than designing and grading tests. Applying for a job as a library assistant in the college library is a far simpler task than seeking an appointment as an assistant professor in a college. Earning a passing grade in a course is a far cry from earning a promotion and tenure status as a faculty member. Learning to get along with one's fellow students is hardly adequate preparation for exerting power as a professor in the political machinations of an academic department. In effect, the skills and perspectives needed to succeed as a professor go far beyond those required to succeed as a student. Thus, the purpose of this book is to explain in detail what the difference is. That aim is pursued by analyzing in detail an array of the most significant contexts inhabited by faculty members in higher education institutions.

A glance at this book's table of contents reveals that among the described settings the classroom context is described only briefly. The reason is that we consider professors' teaching role so vital and so complex that it warrants an entire book of its own. Thus, we have written *A Guide to College and University Teaching* (Iding and Thomas, in press) that serves as a companion volume to *Becoming a Professor*.

THIS BOOK'S STRUCTURE

The chapters that follow this initial chapter are presented within three types of contexts—a preparatory phase ("Preparing to Become a Professor"), an on-the-job phase that addresses research/creativity, teaching, and service roles ("On-the-Job: Research/Creativity, Teaching, and Service Roles"), and a third set of contexts that deals with other influential issues that can affect faculty members' success ("Influential Issues"). The preparatory phase consists of (a) a person discovering kinds of institutions and types of positions in those institutions that might suit his or her talents and interests and (b) ways to enhance one's chances of being hired. The on-the-job phase comes after an individual has been hired and is endeavoring to prosper as a productive member of academia. Influential issues include legal areas, professorial politics, and tenure and promotion. A final chapter addresses higher education's future.

The "Preparing to Become a Professor" phase is described in four chapters.

Chapter 2 ("Types of Higher Education Institutions") identifies types of higher education institutions, along with each type's defining characteristics and its advantages and disadvantages for candidates who might consider applying for a position.

Chapter 3 ("Types of Teaching Positions") identifies kinds of teaching positions within post-secondary institutions, including each kind's advantages and shortcomings.

Chapter 4 ("Profiting from Graduate School") explains ways you can prepare yourself, while still in graduate school, to land the sort of job you desire.

Chapter 5 ("Search Committees, CVs, Interviews, and Job Talk") traces the process of applying for a teaching position and of performing successfully when you are interviewed for a position.

"On-the-Job: Research/Creativity, Teaching, and Service Roles" describes faculty members' responsibilities in the three contexts:

Chapter 6 ("Publishing, Performing, and Products") describes ways that research and creativity are assessed at universities and how faculty members can promote their development as scholars.

Chapter 7 ("Teaching") suggests ways to prepare to teach in higher education, and to improve teaching as one grows as an instructor.

Chapter 8 ("Service Obligations") summarizes the service role that college faculty members are expected to play within the institution, in the surrounding community, and in the scholarly profession at large. The chapter also suggests ways to balance one's service obligations in relation to one's teaching and scholarly pursuits.

"Influential Issues" describes areas about which faculty members should be knowledgeable in order to function well in the above phases.

Chapter 9 ("Ethical and Legal Concerns") explains a variety of moral and legal concerns that have become increasingly prominent in colleges and universities in recent decades—conflicts of interest, intellectual property rights, copyright and fair use, and more.

Chapter 10 ("Professorial Politics") focuses on professors' careers within a political setting when the term political is defined as "the exercise of power." Faculty members, along with support staff, are constantly engaged in efforts to gain power that equips them to fulfill their ambitions in academia. This chapter analyzes sources of power, describes a model of political interaction, offers illustrative cases, and suggests ways that new appointees to a faculty can promote their welfare within such a political environment.

Chapter 11 ("Promotion and Tenure") explains the factors that typically influence a faculty member's chances of being promoted up the hierarchy of ranks, including how promotion is linked to the awarding of tenure that ensures a professor's job security.

As a postscript, chapter 12 ("The Future: Careers in Higher Education") speculates about the future of careers in the professoriate.

CONCLUSION

The dual purpose of this opening chapter has been (a) to suggest why the typical college graduate, despite years spent in classrooms and pursuing online courses, will fail to understand so many of the critical aspects of a career in higher education and (b) to identify the theme of each of the following chapters that are designed to clarify for readers the nature of those critical aspects. As readers progress through the chapters, they will recognize that we have infused the pages with a host of institutional examples that illustrate issues with which college and university faculty members are obliged to contend.

I

Preparing to Become
a Professor

TWO

Types of Higher Education Institutions

When you contemplate pursuing a teaching career in a college or university, you may find it useful to consider the range of institutions from which you might choose. To aid you with this task, the following pages describe a typical variety of institutions.

Post-secondary institutions can profitably be viewed from eight vantage points that could influence your choice of a place to teach. Those vantage points concern an institution's (a) title and structure, (b) mission, (c) reputation, (d) accreditation, (e) sponsorship, (f) size, and (g) location.

INSTITUTIONS' TITLES AND STRUCTURES

Higher education institutions usually bear such titles as college, university, institute, academy, or school, with the title conveying a general idea an institution's structure and purpose.

Colleges

In the United States, liberal arts colleges originated as four-year undergraduate institutions that provide a wide breadth of general knowledge. These colleges (also called colleges of letters and sciences) generally do not offer specific training in vocations, although some provide advanced degrees. Such colleges consist of academic departments—

biology, philosophy, chemistry, English, psychology, mathematics, and more.

Instead of providing broad backgrounds, other colleges provide two-year training for students in specific vocations, hence vocational or trade schools. For example, there are colleges focused on nursing, business, agriculture, and other fields.

Junior colleges generally offer two-year programs of study resulting in associates of arts (A.A.) or associates of science (A.S.) degrees, in liberal arts or vocational areas. Some examples include early childhood education, nursing, criminal justice, business administration, and computer science.

Universities

A university typically provides graduate and undergraduate degrees in a wider range of subjects. It is usually arranged into different schools or colleges, each of which has various academic departments.

In terms of organization, one university may consist of (a) an undergraduate college of letters and science, (b) a college of engineering, (c) a college of creative studies, (d) a school of environmental science, and (e) a graduate school of education. Another university may comprise (a) a college of arts and sciences, (b) a college of architecture and planning, (c) a college of engineering and applied science, (d) college of music, (e) school of business, (f) school of education, (g) school of journalism and mass communication, and (h) school of law. Numerous other combinations of colleges and schools distinguish one university from another.

A present day university frequently has evolved from some simpler form of higher learning institution or even from a secondary school.

The oldest American university, Harvard, was founded in 1638 as Harvard College, intended to educate ministers. There were only nine students in its 1642 graduating class. Currently, Harvard is comprised of twelve colleges and schools, and an Institute of Advanced Study, with a total enrollment of over 20,000 students (Harvard University, 2014).

In many cases, the original school was designed to train teachers in a one or two-year program, then over the years expanded to more advanced years of study and to a wider selection of academic disciplines and vocational fields. For example, University of Northern Colorado originated in 1889 as a two-year State Normal School. In 1911, it was renamed Colorado State Teachers College when a four-year bachelor-of-arts program was introduced. The name changed again in 1935 to Colorado State College of Education. In 1957 the school was renamed Colorado State College when fields of study other than teaching were introduced. In 1970 the college became the University of Northern Colorado with an increasingly extensive curriculum (University of Northern Colorado, 2013).

Another group of institutions from which many of today's universities originated are the agriculture-and-mechanical colleges (also known as land-grant colleges) established for the individual states by the Morrill Acts of 1862 and 1890. In that legislation, the United States Congress awarded federal land to every state to fund a college designed "to teach agriculture, military tactics, and the mechanic arts as well as classical studies so that members of the working classes could obtain a liberal, practical education" (Washington State University, 2009). Today, most of those colleges are universities. The names of some still reflect the original A&M intent of the land grants (Texas A&M University, Alabama A&M University), whereas many others are now known by such titles as University of Arizona, Michigan State University, and Ohio State University.

In summary, universities are usually the most complex types of higher education institutions, with the majority of them tracing their origins to simpler forms of schooling.

Institutes

Institutes in higher education often provide technical studies, especially in such applied areas of the sciences as technology and engineering. Two of the best-known examples are California Polytechnic State University and the Massachusetts Institute of Technology. Other institutes have social science, art, or humanities emphases. Examples include the U.S. Defense Foreign Language Institute, Brooks Institute of Photography, and the Art Institute of Boston.

Academies

At the higher education level, academies provide training in various specializations. These specializations are often in the arts—dance, music, or in military science, such as the U.S. Naval Academy.

Schools

A school in higher education may be a standalone entity, such as the New School in New York, Manhattan School of Music, Julliard School, or the Massachusetts School of Professional Psychology. More often, however, a school is part of a university, as is a college. Examples include a school of education, a medical school, or a law school.

INSTITUTIONS' MISSIONS

The term mission, as used here, means the official purpose that the college or university is intended to serve. The easiest way to find the mission is to enter the institution's name into a web search. The resulting webpage usually offers a section that is entitled "about us" that will include a mission statement. Here are some examples:

> Marion Military Institute, a two-year public [Alabama] institution, educates and trains the Corps of Cadets in order that each graduate is prepared for success at four-year institutions, including the service academies, with emphasis on providing intellectual, moral-ethical, physical-athletic, and leadership development experiences in a military environment. (Marion Military Institute, 2013)

> Like all great research universities, Yale has a tripartite mission: to create, preserve, and disseminate knowledge. Yale aims to carry out each part of its mission at the highest level of excellence, on par with the best institutions in the world. Yale seeks to attract a diverse group of exceptionally talented men and women from across the nation and around the world and to educate them for leadership in scholarship, the professions, and society. (Yale University, 2013)

> The mission of The Juilliard School is to provide the highest caliber of artistic education for gifted musicians, dancers, and actors from around the world, so that they may achieve their fullest potential as artists, leaders, and global citizens. (Juilliard School, 2013)

> The mission of the California Institute of Technology is to expand human knowledge and benefit society through research integrated with education. We investigate the most challenging, fundamental problems in science and technology in a singularly collegial, interdisciplinary atmosphere, while educating outstanding students to become creative members of society. (Caltech, 2013)

Oklahoma State University is a multi-campus public land grant educational system that improves the lives of people in Oklahoma, the nation, and the world through integrated, high-quality teaching, research, and outreach. The instructional mission includes undergraduate, graduate, technical, extension, and continuing education informed by scholarship and research. The research, scholarship, and creative activities promote human and economic development through the expansion of knowledge and its application. (Oklahoma State University, 2013)

The mission of the University of Michigan is to serve the people of Michigan and the world through preeminence in creating, communicating, preserving, and applying knowledge, art, and academic values, and in developing leaders and citizens who will challenge the present and enrich the future.

The University of Michigan intends:

- To be a source of pride for all people of Michigan and have a place in the heart of each member of the University community.
- To have a place in the dreams of every potential member of the community of students, staff, and faculty
- To be recognized as a University that honors human diversity.
- To be a scholarly community in which ideas are challenged, while people are welcomed, respected, and nurtured.
- To be an institution whose environment fosters creativity and productivity among all faculty, staff, and students.
- To occupy a position of unique leadership among the nation's universities in research and scholarly achievement.
- To be a community whose members all share responsibility for supporting its mission and receive recognition for their contributions. (University of Michigan, 1992)

In summary, knowing a college's or university's intended purpose can be useful for helping you decide if that mission is one with which you would like to be associated.

Institutions' Reputations

We imagine that you would like to join an organization that is admired. Therefore, the prestige of a college or university becomes important in your choice of where to teach.

Reputation is a multifaceted characteristic that can be judged from various vantage points, including those of (a) for whom a school's status is important, (b) the features on which the status focuses, and (c) the sources of the reputation.

For whom is an institution's reputation important?

The esteem in which a college or university is held is significant for at least three sorts of people — (a) you as a job applicant, (b) those who judge your acceptability as a job applicant, and (c) others whose opinions you respect.

You yourself. It seems likely that you would prefer to teach in a school that is esteemed by others, because that connection suggests that you — like the institution's other faculty members — are a person of high quality. In effect, you bask in the reflected glory of your school's envied status.

Those who judge you as a job applicant. When you seek a college teaching position, the people who make hiring decisions at the college to which you apply are going to be interested in where you earned your degrees and where you have been previously employed. The more favorable the reputation of your past institutions in the eyes of the decision-makers, the better your chance of getting the job.

Others whose opinions you respect. You probably value the admiration of relatives and acquaintances that you can win by your teaching in a college that they hold in high regard.

A Reputation for What?

An institution's reputation can be general or specific. A general reputation is expressed in global comments like "I understand it's a fine school" or "It's not well known. I've never heard of it." A specific reputation is reflected in comments that apply solely to a particular aspect of the institution, such as:

"I know nothing about their academic program but they have a terrific football team."

"They're known as top-notch in cultural anthropology."

"I hear that their political science department is pretty left wing.

Therefore, as you consider institutions in which you might teach, you may profit from discovering the reputation of the department in which you would be located.

Sources of Reputations

There are various ways to learn about the esteem people assign to a college. Friends may offer their opinions, you may read about the school in a periodical or hear about it on a television program, or you may search for information on the Internet.

Among the most frequently consulted sources are published studies that compare schools by a series of criteria. Consider, for example, the *U.S. News* rankings of close to 1,800 U.S. higher education institutions (U.S. News Staff, 2014a). Although the compilation is designed as a guide to high school students for selecting a suitable college to attend, the information is useful as well to individuals interested in teaching in higher education. One can also find a ranking of graduate schools (U.S. News Staff, 2014b). Additional books of the same sort are *The Best 378 Colleges* (Princeton Review, 2014), which ranks schools in sixty-two categories, and the *Fiske Guide to Colleges* (Fiske, 2014) that rates 310 institutions.

A variety of ratings of academic departments within institutions can be discovered on the Internet by using such descriptors as ranking psychology departments, ranking medical schools, ranking college sports programs, and the like.

However, you should recognize that such rating systems are not without their critics. For example, Reed College stopped contributing data in 1995 to the U.S. News rating project when Reed's president, Stephen Koblik, informed the periodical's editorial staff that he did not find the ranking project credible:

> Reed participated in the survey until 1995, when a front-page article in the *Wall Street Journal* revealed that many colleges were manipulating the system—some by "massaging" their numbers, others by outright fabrication. In the wake of these reports, Steven Koblik, then-president of Reed, informed the editors of USN that he didn't find their project credible and that the college would not be returning any of their surveys—the unaudited questionnaires that form the basis of USN's ranking system. (Reed College Admission, 2014)

In a similar spirit of doubt, Stanford University's president, Gerhard Casper, in 1996 wrote to the editor of *U.S. News*, saying that

> I am extremely skeptical that the quality of a university—any more than the quality of a magazine—can be measured statistically. However, even if it can, the producers of the *U.S. News* rankings remain far from discovering the method. Let me offer as prima facie evidence two

great public universities: the University of Michigan–Ann Arbor and the University of California–Berkeley. These clearly are among the very best universities in America—one could make a strong argument for either in the top half-dozen. Yet, in the last three years, the U.S. News formula has assigned them ranks that lead many readers to infer that they are second rate: Michigan 21-24-24, and Berkeley 23-26-27. (Casper, 1996)

In summary, colleges' reputations, as reflected in published surveys, may be of some use in your effort to estimate the level of esteem that people assign to such institutions, but the survey results may well fail to reflect the qualities you most value in a place to teach.

ACCREDITATION

The term *college accreditation* refers to the practice in higher education of institutional appraisal conducted by external entities that evaluate whether they meet particular standards of quality. Programs, universities, or colleges that successfully pass an accreditation review made by an accrediting body are considered accredited.

When an institution is advertised as accredited, you may wish to learn what agency has done the appraisal and whether the agency is trustworthy. The most comprehensive source of information about such matters is the website titled Financial Aid for Postsecondary Students: Accreditation in the United States (U.S. Department of Education, 2013, para. 3).

However, the Secretary of Education is required by law to publish a list of nationally recognized accrediting agencies that the Secretary determines to be reliable authorities as to the quality of education or training provided by the institutions of higher education and the higher education programs they accredit. . . . The recognition process involves not only filing an application with the U.S. Department of Education but also review by the National Advisory Committee on Institutional Quality and Integrity, which makes a recommendation to the Secretary regarding recognition. The Secretary, after considering the Committee's recommendation, makes the final determination regarding recognition. The U.S. Secretary of Education also recognizes State agencies for the approval of public postsecondary vocational education and State agencies for the approval of nurse education. These agencies must meet the Secretary's criteria and procedures for such recognition and must undergo review by the National Advisory Committee (U.S. Department of Education, 2013, para. 3).

The most direct way to learn the current accreditation status of an institution is to enter the school's name and the word "accreditation" into an Internet search engine, such as Cuesta College accreditation or University of Idaho accreditation.

It is useful to recognize that colleges may be advertised as accredited when such status is not based on an assessment by one of the nation's six regional accreditation agencies that appraise schools and colleges, such as The Middle States Association of Colleges and Schools that appraises post-secondary institutions in Delaware, District of Columbia, Maryland, New Jersey, New York, Pennsylvania, Puerto Rico, the Virgin Islands. For example, other institutions can be state licensed, but not endorsed by a regional agency.

SPONSORSHIP

The organizers and controllers of higher education institutions can be of various sorts, including a government (federal, state, county, city), a religious denomination, a secular group, or an individual person. As you search for colleges in which you might wish to teach, you can learn about institutions' sponsors so as to estimate how closely their mission, source and size of financial support, and philosophical/political atmosphere (liberal, conservative, mixed) match your own preferences.

Usually you can learn an institution's source of sponsorship, mission, and financial condition by entering the school's name into an Internet search, then selecting among the revealed websites to learn the institution's history, form governance, mission, financial resources, and student admissions information.

SIZE

Colleges and universities vary dramatically in size. Consider, for example, student enrollment in the following schools in 2013:

University of California—Berkeley	36,204
Stanford University	18,136
Tufts University	10,819
Brandeis	3,599*

At the undergraduate level, the most populous institutions are likely to have some very large classes—five hundred or six hundred students in a large lecture hall. Those students are often divided into groups of twenty or thirty for supplementary instruction by teaching assistants who are usually graduate students, typically with no formal training as teachers. Less populous schools tend to have far smaller undergraduate classes.

At the graduate level, classes in both large enrollment and small enrollment institutions are far more limited in size.

LOCATION

Collecting information about a college's physical and social environments can help you decide how well such a location would suit your preferred lifestyle. The Internet can provide the information you seek about such features as (a) the surrounding population size and density, (b) seasonal weather conditions, (c) housing costs, (d) food prices, (e) recreational opportunities, and (f) crime rates.

As you plan a teaching career, you may envision your future as a series of phases that could involve, at some particular time, moving from one institution to another so as to progressively improve your circumstances. You might want to start with one type of college and later move to a different type that offers different opportunities or greater challenges.

NOTE

*University size found in Brandeis, 2014; University of California–Berkeley, 2013; Stanford University, 2014; Tufts, 2014.

THREE

Types of Teaching Positions

Just as institutions can be seen from different vantage points, so also can the kinds of teaching jobs in those places. The general nature of college teaching positions has been described in the following manner:

> Postsecondary teachers instruct students in a wide variety of academic and vocational subjects beyond the high school level. Most of these students are working toward a degree, but many others are studying for a certificate or certification to improve their knowledge or career skills. Postsecondary teachers include college and university faculty, postsecondary career and technical education teachers, and graduate teaching assistants. Teaching in any venue involves forming a lesson plan, presenting material to students, responding to students' learning needs, and evaluating students' progress. In addition to teaching, post-secondary teachers, particularly those at 4-year colleges and universities, perform a significant amount of research in the subject they teach. They also must keep up with new developments in their field and may consult with government, business, nonprofit, and community organizations. (Edvisors, 2013)

There are many possible kinds of appointments for college teachers. Consider, for example, this mind-boggling partial list of teaching positions at Harvard University (2011):

> University Professor, Professor (with or without an endowed chair), Professor in Practice (with or without an endowed chair). Associate Professor (with or without an endowed chair), Assistant Professor (with or without an endowed chair), Convertible Instructor, Adjunct Associate Professor, Adjunct Assistant Professor. Professor of Practice

(with or without an endowed chair), Professor in Residence, (with or without an endowed chair), Professor Post-Tenure, Multi-Year Adjunct Professor, Clinical Professor, Associate Clinical Professor, Assistant Clinical Professor, Senior Lecturer, Multi-Year Lecturer, Senior Preceptor, Preceptor, Instructor, Adjunct Professor, Visiting Professor, Visiting Associate Professor, Visiting Assistant Professor, Visiting Professor of Practice, Annual Lecturer, Visiting Lecturer, Clinical Lecturer, Adjunct Lecturer, Non-convertible Instructor, Clinical Instructor, Adjunct Instructor, Clinical Assistant.

And that list does not include the position of teaching assistant, which is often the job in which graduate students gain their first college teaching experience.

To describe all of the types of jobs and their features is far beyond the scope of this chapter. Thus, the following list is limited to five common varieties: (a) professorships, (b) clinical professorships, (c) lectureships, (d) part-time positions, and (e) teaching assistantships.

PROFESSORSHIPS

In particular, professor as a specialized title within the United States refers only to persons whose positions in higher education are officially considered to be on the academic ladder at their institutions. The academic ladder typically includes steps or positions ranging from assistant professor proceeding on up to associate professor and finally, to professor (or full professor), the highest rank. In general, people who choose a teaching career in higher education prefer a position on the ladder to such other sorts as a lectureship, adjunct professorship, or teaching assistantship. The preference is usually based on three features of ladder status—task expectations, job security (tenure), and income. Information about these features at each step of the ladder for a particular institution is often found by entering the name of the institution into an Internet search, followed by such a term as *promotion* or *faculty job description* or *teaching job description* or *teacher employment requirements*.

Task Expectations

In many four-year colleges, and in virtually all universities, faculty members' jobs call for excellent performance in three areas—(a) research and creative activity, (b) teaching, and (c) service. The relative importance of the areas can differ from one institution to another, as reflected in how the three are weighted when faculty members are being considered for promotion to a higher rank. For example, at Duke University, research and scholarly activity is paramount:

> Persons holding the rank of associate professor with tenure are expected to stand in competition with the foremost persons of similar rank in similar fields and to show clear evidence of continuing excellence in scholarly activity in their years at the university. Good teaching and university service should be expected but cannot in and of themselves be sufficient grounds for tenure. The expectation of continuous intellectual development and leadership as demonstrated by published scholarship that is recognized by leading scholars at Duke and elsewhere must be an indispensable qualification for tenure at Duke University. (Duke University, n.d.)

At Boise State University,

> Teaching and scholarly activities . . . represent the most significant elements of the faculty's mission. . . . Service, although expected of every candidate, cannot be considered in place of or substituting for teaching and/or scholarly activities. (Boise State University, 2013, para. 2)

In the chemistry department at the State University of New York's College in Brockport,

> we have the success of our students as our highest priority. Therefore, effectiveness as a teacher shall be weighted as 50 percent. . . . Contributions in "scholarship" and "service" by members of our faculty are co-equal in importance. (State University of New York, College at Brockport, 2011)

What constitutes *research and creative activity* can differ from one department to another. In an English department, it could mean publishing insightful critiques of authors, past or present, in such an academic periodical as the *Modern Language Journal*. Or the contribution might be writing a serious novel or book of poems. In a physics department, the activity could take the form of an article about quarks in the *American Journal of Physics*. In a music department, the creative activity could involve composing a sonata for a string quartet, or it might consist of performing on an instrument—such as the flute or harpsichord—in a concert hall. In an economics department, research could be an analysis of Keynesian theory in the *American Economic Review*. In an education department, the contribution could be a book, issued by a university press, on ways teachers cope with diverse ethnic groups in classrooms. In a fine arts department, an esteemed sculpture, a set of ceramic vases, or a published biography of a famous artist could suffice.

In chapter 2 we noted that, in the growth of American higher education, two-year colleges often evolved into four-year colleges which then added graduate studies to their undergraduate programs. Ultimately they expanded their fields of study to become universities. Under such a pattern of development, the task expectations for ladder faculty members changed. Institutions that had traditionally featured teaching as their main function now placed increasing emphasis on research and scholarship that would result in public displays of faculty members' worth, such as articles in academic journals, books from academic publishers, and artistic performances in prominent venues. This trend has not meant that there are no institutions today that valorize and reward good teaching. Many private liberal arts colleges and public community colleges make teaching their top priority. However, the general trend in an increasing number of public and private universities has been toward making research and creative activity essential for a faculty member to prosper. Hence the phrase "publish or perish."

There are obvious reasons that institutions may stress research and creative activity. First is the matter of evidence about a faculty member's talents. Information about the quality of professors' teaching is often restricted to students in the professors' classes or to members of the professor's department. In contrast, the quality of an individual's research and creative activity is available to colleagues throughout the world—and sometimes to the general population—in the form of journal articles, books, the Internet, or public performances. In effect, those who publish and perform admirably gain fame. Second, it's to a university's advantage to have esteemed scholars on its faculty. The greater the number, the more prestigious the institution. And the greater the college's prestige, the more attractive it becomes to talented students. The larger the pool of talented students seeking admission, the more selective the college can be in accepting ones who will achieve at a high level and, after graduation, become successful in the eyes of the world. Consequently, ambitious higher education institutions are always on the lookout for talented scholars that they might add to their faculty. Ergo, professors who publish or perform publicly in an admirable fashion enjoy more attractive job opportunities and faster promotion than ones who do not.

This advantage that published individuals hold over unpublished ones is frequently criticized as unfair on the grounds that the chief function of a higher education institution should be that of educating its students. Good teaching should be the prime focus in the hiring and promotion of faculty members. And it is no secret among students that a much-published professor is not necessarily an effective teacher. But the reality—particularly in universities and colleges eager to improve their reputation—is that publication and public performance trump teaching and service in decisions about whom to hire and to promote.

In summary, as you consider what type of job would best suit your talents and desires, you can profitably learn the task expectations of institutions to which you might apply for employment.

Job security

Ferguson (2007) quotes Wikipedia's (n.d.) description of the purposes of tenure. Thus, in higher education, *tenure* enables faculty members to freely pursue, write about, and discuss topics of research and inquiry. Tenure reduces concerns about reprisals for potential disagreements with the public or with those in power. In the absence of tenure, academicians might limit themselves to popular areas of research and discussion. Thus, having tenure accords professors independence in their research interests and veracity in sharing findings.

> Note that the intent of granting tenure is to protect the academic freedom of faculty so that new ideas can be pursued even though not popular with others, especially powerful people in the political world—and new ideas are almost always controversial. But it is open debate that usually helps validate or, conversely, shoots down an idea. Job security is a secondary issue since having tenure provides some protection to the individual from being disciplined or fired over what is said or being promoted. . . . Once [a faculty member is] granted tenure, this cannot be revoked by the institution without due process, which means that the institution must bear the burden of proof that the faculty member is professionally incompetent or does such things as violates institutional policies, falsifies academic credentials, and several other conditions. (Furgason, 2007, para. 5–8)

In effect, achieving tenure status pretty well ensures a faculty member's job is safe until retirement, so tenure is a much-valued condition. Traditionally, moving up the ladder from an assistant professorship to an associate professorship has been considered the most critical step on the academic ladder because becoming an associate professor usually includes the awarding of tenure. Instructors and assistant professors can be dismissed at any time, leaving them with little or no recourse. In contrast, an institution must go through an arduous, hazardous legal process to dismiss a tenured associate professor or full professor.

To put in perspective the move from assistant to associate professor, we pause at this point to inspect the typical four-tier advance up the ladder from instructor to full professor. One concise and fairly representative description of the four steps is the set of guidelines for faculty promotion recommendations in Tennessee public universities. The following is a summary of the standards at each step provided by the Tennessee Board of Regents, (2008):

> *Instructor.* [Instructors are expected to have] (a) Demonstrated ability in instruction and/or service, and/or research, (b) Master's degree from an accredited institution in the instructional discipline or related area (c) Evidence of good character, mature attitude, and professional integrity.
>
> *Assistant professor.* [Assistant professors are expected to have]: (a) Earned doctorate or terminal degree from an accredited institution in the instructional discipline or related area. (b) Demonstrate[d] ability in instruction, and/or service, and/or research, and (c) Evidence of good character, mature attitude, and professional integrity.
>
> *Associate professor.* [Associate professors are expected to have]: (a) Earned doctorate or terminal degree from an accredited institution in the instructional discipline or related area, (b) Documented evidence of high quality professional productivity which may lead to national recognition in the academic discipline, and/or consonant with the goals of the university and of the academic unit to which the faculty member belongs, (c) Documented evidence of ability in instruction and/or service and/or research, (d) Evidence of good character, mature attitude, and professional integrity.
>
> *Professor (full professor).* [Full professors are expected to have]: (a) Earned doctorate or terminal degree from an accredited institution in the instructional discipline or related area, (b) Docu-

mented evidence of sustained high quality professional productivity and national recognition in the specified academic discipline that is consonant with the goals of the university and of the academic unit to which the faculty member belongs, (c) Documented evidence of teaching excellence and superior contribution to student development or superior scholarly or creative activity will contribute to the positive record of the candidate for advancement to the rank of professor. Since there is no higher rank, promotion to professor is taken with great care and requires a level of achievement beyond that required for associate professor. This rank is not a reward for long service; rather it is recognition of superior achievement within the discipline with every expectation of continuing contribution to the university and the larger academic community. (d) Evidence of good character, mature attitude, and a high degree of academic maturity and responsibility.

To appreciate the critical nature of the advance from assistant to associate professor, consider the situation that typical assistant professors face. The usual probationary period for assistant professors is six years. Individuals who demonstrate enough promise as productive scholars and teachers during that period will be promoted to the associate professorship and awarded tenure status. Ones who fail to show such promise will be dismissed. This is known as the *up-or-out* policy. Here is the phrasing of the practice at the University of Texas Southwestern Medical Center (2011), where the probationary period is eight years:

Tenure may be withheld on initial appointment to any rank pending satisfactory completion of a probationary period of faculty service not to exceed eight years of full-time academic service. No later than August 31 of the penultimate (seventh) academic year, all nontenured faculty on the tenure-accruing track (and thus accruing time toward satisfaction of the probationary period) shall be given notice that the subsequent academic year will be the terminal year of employment (unless tenure is granted during the eighth academic year). (p. 4)

Exactly what is needed in terms of research productivity at the assistant professor level is sometimes spelled out in detail. For example, consider the promotion requirements in the political science department at the University of North Texas:

Although there are many ways for a candidate to establish a continuous, sustained, and significant scholarly contribution, the publication of six high-quality articles in refereed scholarly journals during the probationary period, at least some of which are of the candidate's sole authorship, will be considered the benchmark for recommendation for tenure. At least two of these articles should appear in general political science journals, as opposed to journals focused on subfields of political science, or belonging to other fields.

In addition to refereed journal publications, the candidate may substitute all other appropriate types of professional activity relevant to the field of political science, including the following:

Publication of a book from a university press or reputable academic publisher.

Publication of book chapters.

Publication of edited books.

Application and acquisition of grants over the review period.

Presentation of papers at professional conferences.

Invited presentations.

Service as a referee, member of an editorial board, or as an editor of a scholarly academic journal.

Important professional activities or recognition (e.g., paper awards) which contribute to the individual's professional stature in the discipline.

Any other types of scholarly publications and efforts which contribute to the candidate's stature in his or her field of specialization. (University of North Texas, Political Science Department, n.d., para. 3–5)

There are individuals who, when they become associate professors, feel that they can now rest on their laurels. With tenure, they are now secure and need not strain to produce more publications or public performances. However, the institutions in which they toil feel differently. Scholarship that earned a candidate tenure is never enough. The phrase "significant continued scholarly contributions" in statements of promotion criteria is not just window dressing. It is intended seriously.

Some faculty members consider the demand for publishing and publicly performing to be a dreaded, unfair burden. Others see it as a welcome challenge, one that is usually accompanied by a lighter teaching load than would be the case if teaching were their primary assignment. Hence, as you ponder the sort of higher education setting in which you would like to work, you can profitably discover what is required to achieve job security in various colleges and universities.

Endowed Chairs and External Grants

Two devices that colleges use to reduce the cost of ladder teaching positions are endowed chairs and external grants.

Endowed chairs

The terms *endowed chair* and *distinguished professorship* refer to faculty positions funded by donations from an individual, a group, a company, or a foundation. The position bears a title chosen by the donor. The title may be the name of (a) the donor or someone in the donor's family (such as the *Mary Clark Rockefeller Chair in Environmental Studies* at Vassar College), (b) a distinguished professor (the *Larry Bell Space Architecture Professorship* at the University of Houston), (c) a group (the *Class of 1941 Memorial Professor of the Humanities* at Clemson University), (d) a foundation (the *C.V. Starr Distinguished Professorship in Finance and Investment Banking* at Hofstra University), (e) the company that gave the money (the *Duke Power Company Distinguished Professor* at Georgia Tech University), or (f) a government (the Norwegian government for the *King Olav V Chair in Scandinavian-American Studies* at St. Olaf College).

The number of endowed chairs can vary markedly from one institution to another. Four example, among the campuses of the University of California in 2011 there were seventy chairs at University of California, Santa Barbara (three of them occupied by Nobel Prize winners), ninety at University of California, Irvine, 110 at University of California, San Diego, and 350 at University of California, Los Angeles (University of California, Irvine, 2011; University of California, Los Angeles, 2011; University of California, San Diego, 2011; University of California, Santa Barbara, 2011). In the California system professors' salaries were paid out of state funds, and the private monies from donations was used for equipment, personnel, travel, and other facilities that supported the chair holder's activities. In many other institutions, the private donations paid all of the professor's expenses, including salary.

Typically, the funds donated for a chair are invested, with the annual income from the investment used to support the professorship. Thus, the original donation continues over the years to finance an academician's work. As a result, the donation needs to be a substantial amount of money. For instance, consider the following appeal to potential donors at

Whitman College, a private four-year liberal-arts institution with an enrollment of around 1,500 students:

> You can make a strategic investment in the faculty and curriculum of
> Whitman College through an endowed chair or professorship in a spe-
> cific academic discipline. A visiting professorship endowment brings
> to Whitman on a rotating basis nationally-recognized scholars or ex-
> perts to provide differing perspectives on academic subject matter. The
> level of support determines the interval and length of visiting professor
> appointments. Endowed funds can also be used to support a perma-
> nent existing faculty position or to create a new position. Each new
> chair or professorship strengthens our traditional disciplines and inter-
> disciplinary endeavors. Minimum for visiting professorship: $1 mil-
> lion. Minimum for permanent professorship: $1.5 million. Minimum
> for permanent chair: $2 million. (Whitman College, 2013)

At another private institution, Stanford University, the cost of a chair
in the late 1990s was $2 million to cover "the costs of a faculty position in
perpetuity. In many cases, it also goes toward defraying expenses related
to the faculty member's work, such as library, secretarial, travel, and
other expenses" (Stanford University News Service, 1997). A decade later
$2.5 million was needed to which $1.5 million from the university was
required to render a total investment of $4 million.

As college costs have risen in recent years, institutions have stepped
up their efforts to acquire more endowed chairs and distinguished professorships.

External grants

At an accelerating pace, colleges and universities have urged faculty
members to attract money in the form of grants from outside the institution to finance research and development activities. The principal sources
of grants are government agencies, philanthropic foundations, and business firms. Wealthy individuals may also provide grant money.

Over recent decades, higher education institutions have grown increasingly enthusiastic over faculty members' obtaining external grants.
In decisions about hiring faulty members and promoting them, a candidate's potential for obtaining grants can loom large. And if you wish to
transfer from one institution to another, your record of obtaining grants
can be an important consideration at the college whose faculty you seek

to join, especially if you already have a grant that would transfer with you.

Professorships in Two-Year Colleges

So far in our discussion of academic ladder positions we have featured four-year institutions and graduate schools. But it is important to recognize that the nation's more than 1,600 community colleges and junior colleges also have ladder professorships with tenure. Ranks can extend from instructor to full professor. In such schools, task expectations focus entirely on teaching, counseling students, and service to the college. Professors are not expected to conduct research, publish, or pursue creative activities that result in public displays or performances. A 2005 survey of junior college faculty members found that 71 percent found meaning and purpose in their work (Evelyn, 2005).

Tenure requirements in two-year colleges have been described by Jenkins (2003) in the following fashion:

> Most community colleges offer some version of tenure [sometimes called a *continuing contract*], and it's often relatively easy to get. Unlike their counterparts at four-year institutions, who may be required to publish numerous articles and perhaps even a book to be considered for tenure, community-college faculty members have no such mandate. The truth is, at most two-year colleges, you don't have to publish anything to get tenure. You will probably be expected to participate in some sort of professional development, but that could mean something as simple as attending technology-training sessions on the campus and going to the occasional academic conference. . . . More importantly, you will certainly have to show evidence of good teaching and also, in most cases, of service to the institution, because those are the primary activities of community-college faculty members. But if you're able to do that—if you can document that you've consistently been a good teacher, that you've served on committees and performed other important functions for the college, and that you've undergone at least some professional development—you can probably get tenure at most two-year colleges in three to five years, seven at the outside. (Jenkins, 2003, p. C1–2)

CLINICAL PROFESSORSHIPS

The title *clinical professor* is assigned to faculty members who are skilled practitioners in such fields as medicine, law, business, psychology, and education. In some institutions, the title *professor of the practice* means the same as *clinical professor*, identifying "distinguished practitioners in their respective professions whose primary responsibilities lie in teaching, mentoring, and service to the university. . . . The teaching, supervising, and mentoring provided is directly related to the *practicum* of the students' programs" (Boston University, 2007, para. 14–16).

Consider, for example, these task descriptions in medicine, law, business, and education.

> *Medical College.* Faculty in the Health Sciences Clinical Professor series teach the application of basic sciences and the mastery of clinical procedures in all areas concerned with the care of patients, including dentistry, medicine, nursing, optometry, pharmacy, psychology, veterinary medicine, the allied health professions, and other patient-care professions. (University of California—Office of the President, 2005, p. 1)

> *Law School.* Members of the Law School's clinical faculty play an important role in the education of our students through their supervision of live client work by students and their teaching in classroom and simulation courses. . . . Clinical faculty may attend all faculty meetings except those dealing with appointment and promotion discussion of research-intensive faculty. Clinical faculty may not vote at faculty meetings. Clinical faculty shall serve on Law School committees if so appointed by the Dean. Clinical faculty shall undertake course assignments and other responsibilities and tasks as assigned by the Dean of the Law School or his or her designate. (Northwestern University School of Law, 2013, para. 2–7)

Business School. This is a segment of a 2009 draft proposal for a clinical faculty track in the Simon Graduate School of Business Administration at the University of Rochester. Clinical professors will be responsible for:

> Teaching undergraduate students and preparing Masters students. . . . Evaluating the effects of innovative policies and practices with the goal of identifying and refining best policies and practices, and making more explicit their connection to existing theories. . . Disseminating the results of own studies and/or of existing theories and research to peers as well as practitioner and policy-making audiences.

Participating in collaborative projects aiming at developing and/or implementing innovative practices and policies.

Providing service . . . to ensure the well-being and good-functioning of the Simon School and the University of Rochester, and one's profession.

Regularly interact[ing] with business institutions and professionals, is current on the issues and problems facing these institutions/professionals, and works with them on significant matters.

Discuss[ing] . . . in an informed way the issues and problems being wrestled with by business institutions, bringing to bear relevant current research.

Identify[ing] what is and is not "quality" research and "wisdom of practice" relevant to specific contexts and goals and as such helps Simon students find, analyze and translate research into practice.

Offer[ing] insights . . .about their own experiences in a way that is relevant to and useful for other professionals in the field and to university-based researchers. (University of Rochester, 2009, p. 7–8)

Education Department. As with all Department of Education faculty, clinical faculty members engage in teaching, service, and scholarship. However, primary responsibilities for clinical faculty are focused on building or maintaining teacher education programs (preservice and inservice) that best serve local, state, national, and international needs. (University of Maryland Baltimore County, 2002, p. 1)

Clinical posts can be either full-time or part-time. Contracts are usually short-term, renewed each year or perhaps at three- or four-year intervals. Appointments typically can be made at any of the traditional four steps on the academic ladder—instructor, assistant professor, associate professor, and full professor. Clinical status rarely includes tenure. Not all clinical positions provide a salary; some are designated *voluntary*— assignments that bear a respected title but no pay. Such posts are usually occupied by individuals who have other sources of income and are willing to dedicate their time and talent to a medical school or business college as a professional responsibility and for the prestige of a professorship title.

LECTURESHIPS

In the United States, the title *lecturer* is usually held by college faculty members who teach full-time or part-time, who bear no research or creative performance responsibilities, and who seldom have tenure. They can be either permanent faculty members or short-term visitors. Lecturers are typically expected to hold a master's degree, but preferably a doctorate or its equivalent. Occasionally an individual who holds less than a master's degree but has a noteworthy record of success in a particular profession or field of knowledge will be appointed to a lectureship.

Various kinds of academic qualifications and task expectations for lecturers are illustrated in the following advertisements for faculty positions:

> *Distinguished Lecturer—Chemistry.* The Chemistry and Biochemistry Department seeks an outstanding teacher and researcher for a Distinguished Lecturer position. The successful candidate is expected to teach large lectures, design new curricula, and lead an undergraduate research laboratory. . . . Qualifications [include] a bachelor's degree in Chemistry is required; PhD in Chemistry preferred. Four years of lecture experience in Chemistry or Biochemistry. One year teaching an ultra-large or jumbo class (more than 500 students). Experience leading undergraduate research projects. Preference will be given to candidates who have a clear record of outstanding teaching, demonstrated student success with large lectures, integrated technology in the lecture hall and assessed its effectiveness, and led undergraduates in successful research projects. (Hunter College, 2013)

> *English Lecturers.* Lecturers teach first-year and advanced writing courses, including courses in writing for the humanities, the social sciences, the sciences, the health professions, and the criminal justice professions. . . . Qualifications [include a] PhD or appropriate terminal degree in Rhetoric and Composition or related field required at the time of appointment. Experience or training in teaching ESL /ELL or working with new and digital media especially welcome. (Northeastern University, 2013)

> *Women's Studies Lecturers.* The successful candidate should be prepared to teach the required introductory Women's and Gender Studies course, Women, Gender Identity, and Ethnicity, and courses such as Introduction to Queer Studies, and Advanced Readings in Queer Studies. Minimum qualifications [include] PhD in Women's and Gender Studies or related field in the Social Sciences or Humanities, completed by August 2014. Preferred qualifications [include] Candidates should have a passion for teaching and a research agenda that informs classroom pedagogy and practice. Preference will be given to candidates with training and expertise in Queer Studies to help build our new Queer Studies minor. Preference is also given to candidates with expe-

rience, ability, and interest in employing feminist pedagogy in the teaching of large and small classes, and evidence of teaching and service with an intersectional framework and to candidates committed to diversity and to working with other faculty members and student groups in and outside the classroom. (Northern Arizona University, 2013)

As these sample cases illustrate, the qualifications and task requirements for lectureships in different institutions can vary widely. So can lecturers' earnings. The American Association of University Professors' survey in 2008 reported the average lecturer salary nationwide as $50,215 (Jaschik, 2008). However, at some of the more prestigious universities, the average is higher and the range is very wide. For instance, according to one salary scale at University of California, Berkeley, lecturers' annual salaries for the year 2011 were projected to range from $44,636 to $135,602, depending on an individual's qualifications, length of service, and field of specialization (UC Berkeley, 2009).

Adjunct Professorships

An *adjunct professor* is a part-time teacher considered to be a temporary employee in a college or university. Appointees may be persons who have a job outside the institution and can bring special skills in a field needed by the institution, or they may be people hired to teach undergraduate classes on a short-term temporary or renewable contract. The number of classes can vary. The pay is usually well below that of tenure-track faculty.

Over the past four decades, the proportion of adjunct faculty in American higher education has risen dramatically as a result of hiring policies designed by college administrators to reduce the cost of instruction. As Bradley (2004) explained, by the end of the 1960s less than 5 percent of faculty appointments were non-tenure track. Further, according to Hoeller (2007), "tenured and tenure-track faculty have dropped from 56.8 percent of the nation's professors in 1975 to 31.9 percent in 2005. In 2005 there were 414,574 tenure and tenure-track professors and 885,803 full-time non-tenure-track and part-time faculty" (para. 11).

For administrators, hiring adjuncts and other part-time or temporary appointees may be appealing, as it is less expensive to hire employees for whom no benefits need to be paid. Furthermore, it is easier to downsize with non-tenured employees. This trend has resulted in a shortage of tenure-track opportunities for qualified candidates. As Bradley (2004) has suggested, this is not just a matter of "supply and demand" because "the same institutions both manufacture and consume the PhD product. There are too few tenure-track jobs for all the PhDs in some disciplines because graduate students or faculty on fixed-term or part-time appointments teach so many courses. If full-time tenure-track faculty taught most courses, there might not be a job shortage" (p. 29).

Adjunct faculty in some states have effectively reacted against this trend by means of legislative lobbying, the court system, and collective bargaining processing (Bradley, 2004). As an example, in 2001 the state legislature of California passed a resolution involving increasing the California State University system's percentage of tenure-track and tenured faculty to 75 percent over eight years (Bradley, 2004).

In summary, there are several advantages to adjunct professorships. First, many such positions are available, many are part-time appointments that can supplement a person's regular employment, and they can serve as an entry-level higher education job in which an individual samples college teaching as a career choice. However, those advantages are accompanied by such drawbacks as a lack of job security and lower pay than tenure-ladder positions offer.

TEACHING, GRADUATE, AND RESEARCH ASSISTANTSHIPS

In higher education, a teaching assistant is typically a college student hired to help professors with their classes. However, teaching assistants sometimes do not function merely as aides but perform the entire instructional role—plan the course content, give lectures, lead discussions, read students' assignments, and give tests. Graduate students who contemplate a college teaching career often find that serving as teaching assistants is a valuable entry step into the profession. Not only does the opportunity enable them to sample the duties that college teaching involves, but having such experience in their record can aid them in getting their first full-time job in academia.

Over recent decades, as college enrollments have grown, so have the numbers of teaching assistantships. As Hoeller (2007) explained, "Student enrollments increased by 60 percent from 1975–2005. And the number of graduate teaching and research assistants grew from 160,606 to 298,602 in the same period" (Hoeller, 2007, para. 7).

The nature of assistantships at different institutions is typically described under the institution's website or on the departmental or college's website. In some institutions, teaching assistantships are called graduate assistantships. To make sure you are knowledgeable about current positions, you should let your advisor, the graduate chair, and department secretary know that you are looking for such a position. Thus, if one is advertised on a listserv to which they subscribe, the information will be forwarded to you.

The task expectations for teaching assistantships are sometimes described in a special handbook, as in this passage from such a publication at the University of Southern California where the job involves:

> Reading course texts and materials, attending lectures, assisting during lectures, leading discussion sections or lab meetings, guiding and monitoring lab exercises, and grading course assignments and exams. Teaching Assistants are expected to hold regular office hours, to respond to student concerns in a responsible manner, and to act as a liaison between the instructor and the students. In addition, the instructor may also ask the Teaching Assistant to prepare or photocopy course materials, organize and maintain audio/visual materials, procure and operate audio/visual equipment, and proctor quizzes and exams. (USC Dornsife, College of Letters, Arts, and Sciences, 2014, para. 4)

Many universities provide teaching assistant training programs, online handbooks, and other resources that explain in great detail how to do the job properly. For example Michigan State University's Department of Computer Science (n.d.) provides an extensive handbook with detailed instructions for such topics as how to conduct group discussion sessions that follow the lectures given by a professor.

Teaching assistants' incomes vary significantly by institutional type and location and by the requirements of the particular job. Further, compensation may include tuition, a very valuable contribution to one's education, indeed.

Another type of assistantship is a research assistantship. Usually funded through grants, this kind of position enables a graduate student to work on a faculty research project, gain research experience, and often plan a thesis or dissertation project that can be funded or partly funded through the grant.

Available Teaching Positions

When you are searching for a teaching job, you can profitably turn to several sources of information about available openings.

The college or university that you attend will have a job placement office. Typical services offered by placement bureaus are illustrated in the following example.

> Eastern Oklahoma State College's Placement Office provides graduates and current students with job information and assistance in finding positions related to specific academic preparation and personal qualifications. An up-to-date listing of temporary, part-time and full-time job vacancies from businesses, private industry, and social services and government agencies is posted on a "Jobs Board", which is accessible to current students, graduates, and the community.The Placement Office provides assistance with resume writing, interviewing tips and other job-seeking skills, as well as schedules on-campus interviews with businesses, federal/state agencies and public schools. The Placement Office also assists employers in locating qualified persons to fill vacancies in their organizations. Faculty members are extremely involved in locating the most qualified applicant for the vacancy. Students are encouraged to register with the Placement Office so they will be notified of job openings relating to their chosen fields. (Eastern Oklahoma State University, 2014)

The Internet is an excellent source of job openings. First, become familiar with academic job listings, such as those on the *Chronicle of Higher Education* (chronicle.com/section/Home/5) or other listing sites. Entering such descriptors as *college teaching jobs, college employment opportunities,* or *university teaching* into an Internet search will also generate a multitude of available positions. Furthermore, if you belong to a professional association affiliated with your field, or a special interest group within that association, you might register for a job placement service that enables you to receive listings as they are posted. (In chapter 5, we will describe more about the hiring process.)

Professors with whom you have studied sometimes hear of teaching posts in other institutions, so it can be useful for them to know that you hunting for such an opportunity.

Your fellow graduate students who have now completed their studies and have taken teaching jobs may learn of openings in the colleges where they are now located. If they learn that you are job-hunting and they respect your ability, they may inform you of those opportunities.

CONCLUSION

The purpose of this chapter has been to offer a brief overview of typical kinds of teaching positions in American colleges and universities. We have focused primarily on task expectations and required qualifications along with advantages and disadvantages of different types of teaching positions from the viewpoints of job security and income.

FOUR

Profiting from Graduate School

We assume that you are currently attending graduate school, pursuing a master's degree or a doctorate. Or perhaps you are not yet a graduate student but are considering enrolling in a graduate program. In either case, what you do during your graduate studies can critically influence your chances of getting the sort of college teaching job you want. The purpose of this chapter is to describe a variety of ways you can increase your chances of achieving that goal.

The aspects of life in graduate school analyzed in the following pages concern (a) academic achievement, (b) suitable advisors, (c) practical experience, (d) professional organizations, (e) publishing, performing, and products, and (e) politics in academia.

ACADEMIC ACHIEVEMENT

It may appear foolish and redundant of us to suggest that you try your best to do truly excellent work in your graduate courses. That seems obvious. But we don't mean only that your academic record looks better when you earn good grades. Rather, the point is that your chance of getting an excellent teaching job after graduation can be significantly influenced by what your professors in graduate school think of your ability. If the quality of your performance in their classes and seminars is extraordinarily good, they will be enthusiastic to help you get a good job. Their help can take three principal forms. First, they will write convincing letters of recommendation to support your application for teaching positions. Second, they will propose you as a suitable candidate for jobs that come to their attention. Third, they will actively try to discover job openings that would suit your skills and interests.

There are several ways to set yourself above ordinary graduate students. Among the most basic ways are those of (a) submitting assignments on time, (b) going beyond the minimum work needed to barely get by (such as the number of pages, number of references, number of interviews, number of illustrations), (c) writing and speaking fluently, (d) doing well on tests, and (e) not complaining about how the class is conducted. Beyond those basics are others that can draw attention to your initiative, diligence, and talent, such as (f) displaying leadership in group activities, (g) showing sincere enthusiasm for the subject matter of the class, (h) volunteering for special tasks (contributing to the professor's research program, offering to help classmates with their studies), and (i) serving as research assistant or teaching assistant.

Imagine that you are a professor in a college history department and you are asked to serve on a committee that assesses candidates for a new assistant professorship in your department. You are hunting for a bright young scholar who specializes in European history, particularly British history. Here are two letters of recommendation included in the files of a pair of candidates. Each letter is from a professor of history at the university in which each candidate did her graduate studies. Which letter would impress you more favorably?

First letter

This letter is sent at the request of Ms. Chelsea Smith. She was a student in a course I teach titled Rule Britannia, which focuses on British history during the nineteenth and early twentieth century. According to my records, she earned a grade of B in the class.

Second letter

I am writing in support of the application of Sally Smith, who completed her doctoral studies in history at our university. I came to know her well, for she not only enrolled in two of my regular classes (European Revolutions, Britain During the Enlightenment) but she was also a member of an advanced seminar (Elizabethan Times). She did excellent work in each of these settings and later served as one of my research assistants, helping find background material for a book I was working on at the time (Germans on the British Throne). Two of Sally's traits that particularly impressed me were her engaging sense of humor and her ability to come up with unusual, but logical, ways of interpreting historical events. I see her as enjoying a very bright future as a history teacher. The institution that hires her will be fortunate, indeed.

Finally, in your eagerness to attract attention to yourself as an enthusiastic and able scholar, it is useful to recognize the matter of style, with style meaning the manner in which you pursue your goal of improving your job-getting opportunities while in graduate school. Your success will likely be diminished if you appear to be unduly "pushy" and a "know-it-all"—overbearing and tramping on other people's feelings in your effort to appear superior. Your success will likely be greater if you appear to be a friendly, enthusiastic, sincere student and supportive classmate.

SUITABLE ADVISORS

Among the professors you encounter in graduate school, the one who may be the most important for your finding a suitable teaching post is your academic advisor. Or perhaps you will have more than one advisor, with one of them your official mentor and others who serve as unofficial sources of advice. Or possibly you will change official advisors during your time in school. In any case, three characteristics of advisors—compatibility, availability, status in the profession—can determine how useful they will be in your search for a satisfying career in higher education.

Compatibility

At least two aspects of compatibility can be important—sociability and academic agreement. Sociability means how well you and your advisor like each other, that is, enjoy each other's company and treat each other with respect. If you dislike or disrespect each other, then you not only may find life in graduate school rather miserable, but you probably cannot count on your advisor's support in your hunt for a job.

Academic agreement means how closely you and your advisor concur on what you hope to achieve in graduate school and on how you hope to accomplish it. For instance, consider these two situations.

For his master's degree thesis, a student in an anthropology department fervently wishes to study the social organization and customs of Latino immigrants who work as itinerant agricultural laborers on farms and in orchards in Southern California. However, the professor who was assigned as the student's advisor is an archeologist, specializing in the study of pre-Columbian village life of Pueblo Indians in the Southwestern United States. The professor has no interest, and little expertise, in the cultural anthropology of farm laborers. He wants the student to study, instead, pre-Columbian Pueblo pottery, which is an aspect of the archeological digs in which the professor and his research team are currently engaged. So the student faces a choice of either doing the archeologist's bidding or seeking a different advisor, who would be a cultural anthropologist glad to have the student study immigrant farm labor.

A doctoral student in a university physics department wants to specialize in Einsteinian-relativity research but the professor who was assigned as his advisor focuses his own attention primarily on quantum mechanics. The major research funding that the professor commands enables him to hire research assistants at generous salaries. The doctoral student has been offered one of those assistantships, but it means he would need to curtail his concentration on relativity theory. His advisor doesn't object to the student's focusing chiefly on relativity, but then the student would need to turn to other professors as his principal mentors and he wouldn't get the research assistantship.

As in these two cases—and when a professor and a student really dislike each other—students find themselves wondering whether they should change advisors. And if so, how should they go about it. Deftly managing such a task is sometimes easy, but other times it's a risky business, particularly when professors interpret such an attempt as a personal insult that they resent. Hence, we have a few rather obvious suggestions to offer about how to manage a change of advisors.

First, don't shuck off your present advisor before you have a new one who is able and willing to be your chief mentor. If, in a petulant moment, you "tell off" your current advisor and then are unable to find another willing one, you can end up abandoned, with no one to offer guidance and aid.

In your search for a suitable mentor, you could turn to several resources. You might make an appointment with the department chairperson to whom you explain your plight and ask for how to find a new advisor. Or you might consult a faculty member whom you respect and feel comfortable with. Or you could ask the opinion of classmates, particularly ones who have been in the graduate program long enough to understand departmental politics.

Once you have been accepted by a new advisor, the department chairperson may inform your previous advisor of the change. And you may wish to speak to your previous advisor, thanking him or her and explaining as best you can why you sought a different mentor.

Availability

The best sort of advisor is one you can consult whenever you need help. Some professors are so busy that it takes weeks to get an appointment with them. And when you do meet with them, they may seem in such a hurry or appear so distracted that the session fails to solve your problems. Mentors who are opening their mail or taking phone calls while chatting with you are not what you need.

Worse still are faculty members who are rarely on campus. They are on sabbatical leave during the time you are working on your thesis, serving as visiting professors for a semester, traveling abroad, attending conferences, on book-peddling tours, gathering data for their research projects, giving advice to corporations and government agencies, and more. Frequently, such multitasking academicians are famous people, ones whose influence could help get you attractive teaching jobs after you graduate. But while you are working on your thesis or dissertation, they are of little help because they aren't available when you need them.

In effect, when you are selecting an advisor, you may need to decide whether it is more important for you to have the mentor available or to have one who is famous and might be more influential in your getting a favored teaching position after graduation.

Status in the Profession

Three ways that an advisor's professional standing can affect an advisee's appointment to a college teaching position are the advisor's (a) reputation in higher education, (b) professional connections, and (c) publications to which the advisee contributed or co-authored.

In general, the more widely known and respected a professor is, the more readily members of a search committee will trust what the professor writes and says about a teaching job applicant. Thus, receiving enthusiastic support from a renowned scholar can be of considerable value to an applicant.

It can also be helpful for a job hunter to have an advisor with a host of friends in academia, friends who know of attractive job openings and will ask the advisor to recommend prospective candidates.

The most frequent way that academicians gain fame outside their own university is through their publications and performances. Sometimes graduate students' names are attached to such publications and events. An article on polymers in a chemistry journal may carry the professor's name as principal author, with a student's name as one of the coauthors. In a book on economic theories edited by a professor, an advisee may be credited with writing one of the chapters. A professor's article on the genetics of frog species that appears on a biological-science website may include a footnote recognizing the aid of a graduate student. Or the printed program for a concert hall flute performance by a professor may include the name of the student who served as the piano accompanist.

We note that in the social sciences, many applicants have already co-authored papers, often as first author with co-authors, or even as sole author. All such evidence strengthens an applicant's position when applying for a college teaching job.

PRACTICAL EXPERIENCE

Department heads and members of search committees often look with favor on job-candidates whose records include first-hand experience with the "real world of work" that relates to their academic specialization. Such experience is typically acquired before or during the years that students are in graduate school. Thus, job seekers are advised to include evidence of such practical knowledge in their applications for a college teaching post. The following are kinds of practical work related to different academic fields.

- A sociologist was a volunteer aide in a city's shelter for the homeless.
- A civil engineer worked on a road construction crew during summer vacations.
- An English major was a part-time journalist on a small town newspaper.
- A school administration major served as an elementary school teacher's aide.
- A political scientist helped with a state senator's election campaign.

- A computer scientist was a freelance programmer.
- An economics major spent summers working in a brokerage office.
- A kinesiologist was a part-time personal trainer in a fitness center.
- A physical education major coached a junior high basketball team.
- A clinical psychologist volunteered as a counselor in a drug treatment facility.
- An international relations major who served in the Peace Corps.

Professional Organizations

Each academic discipline includes scholarly associations—sometimes called learned societies—whose membership includes individuals who specialize in the discipline, such as professors, graduate students, and enthusiasts in the particular field of knowledge or in an allied vocation. Some disciplines have numerous associations, so the total in all academic fields combined extends into the thousands. Here are a few examples of such groups.

American Institute of Physics
Society for Philosophy and Psychology
National Flute Association
Modern Language Association
Association of American Geographers
Society of American Foresters
Society of Architectural Historians
Society of Biblical Literature
American Geophysical Union
American Statistical Association
Economic History Society
American Medical Association
American Society for Aesthetics
College Art Association
American Classical League
American Anthropological Association
American Society for Neurochemistry
Sports and Entertainment Law Society
Society of Dance History Scholars
Society for Industrial and Applied Mathematics

Students who join an association that is allied to their academic specialization may profit in several ways from their membership and their participation in the organization's activities. Members are usually sent periodic newsletters telling of the group's current events, such as the upcoming national conference and regional conferences. Societies often provide more than one type of membership. Consider, for instance, the regular and student categories in the American Educational Research Association (2013, para. 1–2).

> Regular Members: Eligibility requires satisfactory evidence of active interest in educational research as well as professional training to at least the master's degree level or equivalent.

> Graduate Student Members: Any graduate student may be granted graduate student member status with the endorsement of a voting member who is a faculty member at the student's university. . . . Graduate Student membership is limited to five years.

There are similar requirements for joining societies in a wide range of other academic disciplines, such as the American Society for Biochemistry and Molecular Biology (2014):

> Regular Membership: Available to any individual who holds a doctoral degree and who has published, since receipt of the doctoral degree, at least one paper in a refereed journal devoted to biochemistry and molecular biology. (para. 2)

> Graduate Membership: Available to any graduate student. Graduate members may not vote, hold elective office, nominate new members or sponsor papers by nonmembers at the society's annual scientific meeting. Graduate members are eligible for automatic promotion to regular membership by certifying that they have attained the necessary qualifications. There is a time limit of five years for graduate membership. (para. 4)

In some cases, members receive a periodic journal featuring recent trends in the profession, discussions of controversial issues, and book reviews. For example, in the American Psychological Association,

> Student affiliates get many benefits of full membership, including the Monitor on Psychology, American Psychologist, and gradPSYCH—the magazine for graduate students— as well as special services, and substantial discounts on APA products, including APA's premiere line of electronic databases. . . . Graduate and undergraduate students can become Student Affiliates and members of APAGS, the national organ-

ization representing graduate students in psychology. (American Psychological Association, 2014)

The only requirement for joining some learned societies is proof of current enrollment as a college student. Such is the case of the African Studies Association in which student members' reduced annual fees entitle them to

> a subscription to *African Studies Review*, a multi-disciplinary scholarly journal, which publishes original research and analyses of Africa and book reviews as well as a digital subscription to *History in Africa*, an annual journal that features textual analysis and criticism, historiographical essays, bibliographical essays, archival reports and articles on the role of theory and non-historical data in historical investigation.

- A discounted registration fee to attend the Annual Meeting
- A listing in the ASA Online Membership Directory with an advanced search feature to easily locate ASA colleagues and individuals
- An opportunity to vote to elect officers and members of the Board of Directors
- An opportunity to serve on ASA Committees
- The ability to nominate individuals for the Distinguished Africanist Award. (African Studies Association, 2014)

Other societies have no educational or experiential qualifications for membership. Anyone interested in the organization's mission and activities is welcome. Such is the case with the American Classical League, in which "membership is open to any person who is committed to the preservation and advancement of our classical inheritance from Greece and Rome" (American Classical League, 2014).

In a variety of ways, attending a professional society's national and regional conferences can be a boon for jobseekers. At conferences you can (a) attend lectures and discussion sessions that update your knowledge in your academic specialty, (b) meet professors and students from other universities, (c) learn of job openings and participate in on-site interviews, (d) be interviewed by a college's search committee members, (e) report your own research, and (f) serve on discussion panels. Many societies include sections or special interest groups (SIGs), which focus on particular concerns within the organization's broad domain. For example, by 2014 the American Sociological Association included fifty-two sections bearing such titles as culture, children and youth, economic sociology, family, human rights, and evolution, biology, and society.

> The purpose of sections is to promote the common interest of Association members in specified areas of sociology . . . they are a means of increasing communication and interaction among persons of similar interests within the framework of a larger organization. While sections facilitate relationships and work among persons with a common interest, they also provide an opportunity for individuals to participate actively in their national association. (American Sociological Association, n.d.)

In summary, joining one or more learned societies while in graduate school and participating in the organization's activities can help in several ways to improve a student's chances of finding a satisfactory college teaching job.

PUBLISHING, PERFORMING, AND PRODUCTS

This aspect of a career in academia is usually referred to as research and creative activity. It assumes three main forms—publications, performances, and products. Publishing refers to writings issued in print, especially in books and academic journals. Performing refers to an individual appearing before an audience to deliver a speech, play a musical instrument, act in a theatrical production, or the like. Products are observable items (other than print publications) that a person has created, such as a scientific instrument, oil painting, architectural structure, or computer program.

Later in this book, chapter 6 explains in detail the role of publishing, performing, and creative products in college teachers' careers. Therefore, the following examples are not intended to explain in detail the nature of such activities in higher education. Rather, the examples simply illustrate typical ways that students' publications, performances, and products during their graduate years can strengthen their preparation for job hunting.

- In a footnote on the opening page of a geology journal article, the professor who authored the article named a student assistant who had helped substantially in collecting and analyzing rock specimens on which the article's data were based.

- The printed program for a university-sponsored string quartet concert featured the names of the four students who performed the evening's compositions.
- Among the three coauthors of a chapter titled "A Chicago Neighborhood Council" in a book about social action at the local level, the first two authors were professors, whereas the third was a graduate student.
- The published conference proceedings for the annual convention of an economics association consisted of abstracts and papers presented during the conference, with several of the papers authored by graduate students.
- A graduate student's acrylic painting titled "Cathedral in Morning Mist" was awarded a third place prize in a statewide art exhibition.
- In a literary magazine, a critical review of the book *New Light on Pepys' Diary* was written by a student from a university's English department.
- On a television station's news program, a graduate student from a college's political science department was interviewed about her experiences while working on a presidential candidate's election campaign.
- A graduate student in a college's psychology department publishes a journal article about his study of child-rearing practices in single parent homes. The study had been the focus of his master's degree thesis.
- A psychology department graduate student from Germany wrote a German-language adaptation of the original English language version of a book titled *Recent Theories of Learning*. The original author of the English language edition was the student's academic advisor in an American university. The German edition listed the student as the co-author.

Thus, it is apparent that there are numerous ways that students can compile records of publishing, performing, or products that reflect their initiative in displaying their talents in a public fashion that is valued by the people who make college and university hiring decisions.

POLITICS IN ACADEMIA

At first glance, you might expect that our use of the phrase politics in academia is restricted to broad political issues in the general society, issues that are reflected in such remarks as "that political science department is full of Democrats" or "the economics department is dominated by Republicans and Libertarians" or "those sociologists are mostly bleeding-heart liberals." However, we are using the word political in a far more encompassing manner. For us, the word political means the use of power in any human relationship. We define power by how the presence—physical or psychological—of one person or one group influences the thought and behavior of another person or group. For example, if the presence of Person A (bodily or just in someone's thoughts) affects how Person B feels or acts, then A has power over B. But if the presence of A fails to alter B's thought or action, then A has no power over B. Such power can vary from slight to enormous.

We are suggesting that graduate students are well advised to identify the political conditions—that is, the power relationships—within the institution they attend and, also, when seeking a college teaching post, to try to learn about political conditions in the institutions to which they are applying for a job.

We believe it is useful to view the politics of a higher education institution from two perspectives, those of (a) power and authority, and (b) sources of power.

Power and Authority

As we have proposed, power is the extent to which the presence of one person or one group affects the thoughts and doings of another person or group. We then define authority as "the official power given to a person or group." The president of a college has greater assigned power than a dean. A dean has greater assigned power than a professor. A professor has greater assigned power than a student.

Within a college or university, the extent of different people's authority and the lines along how their power is to be exerted are typically represented in an organizational chart, as in the imaginary small college portrayed in figure 4.1. Larger institutions' authority structures are far more complex. The higher that a position is located on the chart, the greater the power. The lines connecting the positions on the chart represent the channels through which power is exerted downward.

Within the institution's authority structure, a person's job entails both responsibilities and rights. The responsibilities are actions for which a person can be rewarded if carried out properly and can be punished if not performed satisfactorily. The rights or privileges are treatment a person deserves at the hands of an authority. Each person's job description—either written or simply understood by dint of custom—identifies the aspects of life in which his or her position in the organizational structure is empowered to control. A person's job description usually specifies which aspects of life fall with an authority's jurisdiction, with some of those aspects clearly specified (teaching load, research output, service to the department), whereas others are loosely identified by such terms as "common decency." Under "publicly offensive acts" a professor may be remonstrated by a department head for coming to class drunk, but the department chair cannot prevent the professor from drinking at home.

College Authority Structure

The job description may also spell out the rights and privileges of a person's particular position. The protections under college tenure status are an example of such rights. Or if members of a college faculty belong to a labor union, the union contract will usually specify the members' rights and will identify sanctions that will be taken against the college if the rights are breached.

Therefore, when you are investigating a teaching job for which you might apply, you can profitably seek information about what the job's responsibilities and rights will be. Certain of those matters will be in the job description. Others will be in a faculty handbook and in discussions with faculty and support staff, such as secretaries and teaching assistants. Graduate students in an institution are also often useful sources of such information, particularly in the form of gossip about administrators' or professors' unofficial practices that they assume their authority allows.

Sources of Power

People outside of colleges and universities often don't understand that the titles academicians bear may not represent the power they wield within their own institution or in national and international higher edu-

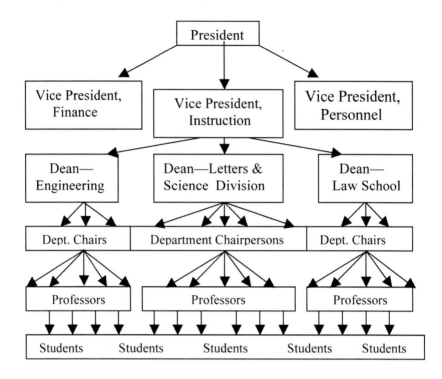

Figure 4.1.   College Authority Structure.

cation circles. Students themselves—particularly undergraduates—are often unaware of who has power over whom in the college they attend. This is because they fail to recognize sources of power other than authority positions, such sources as scholarly prestige and fund-raising skill.

Scholarly Prestige

We are using the expression scholarly prestige to mean an academic's reputation among other academics, particularly among colleagues at institutions across the nation or around the world in the individual's discipline or profession. Such prestige derives from how a biologist is regarded by other biologists, how a computer scientist is assessed by other computer scientists, how a French literature professor is ranked by other French literature professors, and how a surgeon is rated by other surgeons.

Evidence of academics' scholarly quality is almost always in the form of publications and performances—things that are accessible to public appraisal. An anthropologist whose innovative textbook has been adopted widely in North American colleges gains power, because he is widely admired and sought after as a faculty member in colleges that wish to add a luminary to their anthropology department. A composer gains power when her music is performed by respected symphony orchestras. The influence wielded by a political science professor increases when his journal article on states' rights wins an award at the annual convention of the American Political Science Association.

Faculty members with enviable scholarly reputations are able to exert power within their college or university that can be contrary to the authority structure of their institution. The vice president of the college must be very careful about the way she treats the professor of physics who has won a Nobel Prize. The dean of the College of Letters and Science is wise to be generous to the associate professor of English whose recent novel won a Pulitzer Prize. The chair of the Spanish language department, who has published only three journal articles over the past five years, wields less power in departmental affairs than does the member of the faculty who is a much-published editor for a well-respected journal.

A lesson to be drawn from recognizing the power of scholarly prestige is that when you are job hunting, the support of a prestigious professor will carry more weight than an endorsement from either a less eminent professor or from an administrator higher in the authority structure, such as a department chair or dean or provost, whose record of scholarly contributions is undistinguished. Hence, during your years as a graduate student, it is important to impress influential academics with your talent and dedication.

Fund-raising Skill

Faculty members gain power within their university when they attract funding from outside sources—from government agencies, philanthropic foundations, business corporations, and wealthy patrons. The importance of grant getting has grown markedly in recent decades as public funds for higher education have failed to keep up with the costs of higher education. Money from outside enables professors to purchase equipment, carry out research, pay travel expenses, hire staff, expand offices, and add laboratories. Adept grant getters delight administrators, thereby increasing the grant getters' power.

From the standpoint of your securing a college teaching position, the power acquired by a grant getter might open your way to a temporary job that you could work into a permanent instructorship or professorship. Whereas appointments to regular teaching positions usually must go through a rather rigorous process of selection by faculty committees and administrators, grant holders sometimes have the power to choose who joins their projects. That is because the positions are temporary, lasting only as long as the grant continues. But during that period, persons hired with grant funds (soft money, compared to regular-budget hard money) can prove their worth and become favored candidates for a permanent teaching or research post.

For a more detailed discussion of power struggles in academia, see chapter 10: "Professorial Politics."

CONCLUSION

The intent of this chapter has been to identify opportunities in graduate school that can enhance your chances of landing a satisfying college teaching position. We have reviewed those opportunities as they relate to six aspects of the graduate school experience: (a) academic achievement, (b) suitable advisors, (c) practical experience, (d) professional organizations, (e) publishing and performing, and (e) politics in academia.

FIVE

Search Committees, CVs, Interviews, and Job Talk

Suppose you happen to see an advertisement for your "ideal job" on the *Chronicle of Higher Education*'s website or in AcademicKeys.com. You ask friends or professors for sample cover letters and curriculum vitae (CV=one's job qualifications; a resume). Then you create your own CV and send it to the prospective job sites, hoping that you will be one of the lucky people to be invited for an interview, or better yet, offered the job. What determines whether you'll be invited for an interview? Will sending a good CV and cover letter—and preparing for your "job talk"—be enough to tip the scales in your favor over other candidates? What really goes into hiring a new professor at a university or other higher education institution?

In this chapter, we describe a college's typical hiring process, from determining the need for a new position in a department, creating a job advertisement, selecting a search committee, evaluating applications, inviting candidates for on-site interviews, and making final hiring decisions. Through a behind-the-scenes-look, with examples and suggestions about how to best present yourself and your qualifications, we hope to provide the best edge for you as you embark on this important part of your new career in higher education.

The chapter is presented in seven parts: (a) advertising an available position, (b) how to create a stellar CV, (c) how to shine during a telephone interview, (d) interviewing at conferences, (e) how to ace your on-site interviews, (f) how to impress with your job talk, and (g) after the interview.

ADVERTISING AN AVAILABLE POSITION

Most college job openings result from positions being vacated through retirements, faculty members leaving for positions in other institutions, or an increase in student enrollment. And particularly in good economic times, new positions can be allocated in areas that a college or university plans to expand. Consider these situations:

> The accounting and finance section of a state university's school of business advertises an endowed chair position that had been held by a distinguished professor who recently retired due to ailing health. The appointment will be at the associate professor or full professor level. Candidates must have a strong reputation in accounting or finance, an earned doctorate, and a distinguished record of top journal publications.

> To replace a faculty member who left the community college for job at a movie studio, the college hunts for a replacement for the position of Theater Instructor/Program Coordinator whose duties include (a) teaching theater courses, (b) supervising theater technicians to ensure that their facilities are in performance-ready condition, and (c) monitoring the quality of the design, direction, and conduct of theater productions each semester.

> A junior college that plans to launch online classes on water resources wishes to hire an instructor for a full-time, non-tenure-track position. Candidates must have a master's degree in water resources or hydrology and college level online teaching experience.

> A college of education seeks to expand distance education with increased online course offerings, so planners have developed a program in educational technology and now move to hire professors and instructors to staff the program.

The process of identifying the need for a new faculty member usually begins with academic departments assessing their development plans and making requests to the dean of their division who determines how to allocate positions and in what priority. So departments—usually department chairs—make their strongest possible cases for hiring new faculty members. Depending upon available funds and higher administrators' approval, the dean will give a department the go-ahead to conduct a search for suitable candidates.

A search committee is then convened, consisting primarily of department members, the majority of whom are at a rank at least as high as the position being filled. For example, if the position is for an associate professor, most search committee members are at that level or above. If the opening is for a department chair, or the department is a small one, the whole department could be involved. Most committees also have an outside member, a person from another department whose job is to ensure that the procedure is conducted according to university guidelines and regulations.

The committee creates an advertisement, based upon assessing the department's needs and university mandates for positions that might be in operation. For example, an English department might wish to replace a retiring professor who specialized in modern American literature, yet must also give high priority to applicants who have taught in teacher-education programs. You'll note that many ads specify "minimum qualifications" and "desirable qualifications" for positions. How well you meet those qualifications will determine whether your application is quickly moved to the stack that gets a prompt rejection or is kept in another pile for further consideration.

As we examine the advertisement and the stages of the hiring process, let's consider two hypothetical applicants, Janis and Marcus. Marcus is at the all-but-dissertation stage (ABD), meaning that he has passed all of the exams—comprehensive and qualifying—required by his university to allow him to "advance to candidacy" or begin work on his dissertation. Janis has completed her PhD and currently works as a postdoctoral appointee at another university.

Marcus writes a cover letter specific to the position, addressing how his qualifications meet each requirement, both minimal and desirable. Janis figures that since she is applying to a number of institutions and has worked very hard at composing a generic cover letter that was favorably reviewed by her former academic advisor, she will modify a few points to make it more specific to the application and send it in.

Whose application will impress the selection committee? Keep in mind that if you do have specific expertise related to the job you're applying for, you need to make that expertise stand out in your cover letter.

The committee should not have to search for your expertise, going back to transcripts and coursework you have completed to see if you have studied enough in a particular area so that you can teach relevant courses.

Once the applications have been received, they may be held until the application deadline date. Then the committee begins to review applications for narrowing down those that meet the minimum qualifications and those that do not. Some deadlines are more flexible; verbiage like "applications received until position is filled" might appear in the ad. This language enables the committee to continue advertising and interviewing should an employable candidate not readily emerge from the initial set of applications. However, most departments hope to hire candidates soon, not let positions remain vacant for extended times. They need to act quickly to compete for the best candidates, and they also know that while funding may be currently available, it could be withdrawn quickly by administrators in an effort to cut budgets.

The committee—or a subset that usually consists of at least two individuals—then rates the applications for minimal qualifications. Applications that fail to meet minimal qualifications are placed in a "reject" pile. Some applications may be only distantly related, or even unrelated, to the position being advertised. Perhaps the university is one of several in desirable locations and applicants who are doing "mass mailings" submit their applications, much like lottery ticket buyers hope to purchase the winning ticket.

At this point, you might receive a polite rejection letter (or not as some committees might send such letters out when the search is complete). Rejection letters can be helpful in that you are aware that you need to focus your efforts elsewhere. Rejections can also be useful wake-up calls for candidates who are too attached to particular positions.

Next, the committee rates applications that have made it past the preliminary screening. To help make the process as objective as possible, the committee may use a rubric (rating scheme) and assign points in each assessment category. For example, in the category titled "teaching experience," an applicant might receive a higher score if she has taught complete courses in the area that the position is for. Or if she's been only a teaching assistant and has delivered no more than a few guest lectures, she might receive fewer points for teaching experience but is still awarded a positive score.

For "research potential"—which is also a typical category—a candidate might receive a very high score if he has won a dissertation award, presented research at least one major conference, authored or co-authored at least one publication in a highly regarded journal. A candidate will be rated less highly if he has no publications, or if several items listed are "in progress." Similarly, a candidate is seen as showing strong research potential if she has been listed on a publication as the first author or sole author (possible in the social sciences but less likely in the physical sciences) on several publications related to an integrated research area. A candidate may show less initiative if she is listed as a second or third author on disparate publications. Initiative can be important, but institutions that value research hope to hire a faculty member who can add a new or complementary research area and will develop his or her own coursework and guide students in their own related research.

Citing one's awards for excellent teaching or research or other similar distinctions can also strengthen an application, as does service to the profession and community. Perhaps a candidate has been an officer in a professional organization or graduate student organization. Perhaps she has served as a graduate student representative to a faculty committee. Service could be rated as well; however, it may be less essential to hiring decisions, especially if service qualifications are not listed as part of the advertisement. However, a candidate's propensity toward service can tell the committee whether the applicant has leadership qualities, altruistic tendencies related to one's professional life, and potential to participate in departmental and other forms of service required of faculty members. In other words, will the applicant be a good team player and departmental colleague or will she avoid service in order to advance her professional reputation?

Now let's return to our hypothetical candidates. Suppose Marcus has served as teaching assistant for two courses and has taught one class by himself. Janis has never taught but has presented research at conferences and given talks for her research group, talks that are highly regarded, according to her supervisor. If you were serving on the hiring committee, you would need to decide whether Janis' strong background in research will also translate into effective teaching. Our advice to Janis would be to highlight all of her teaching-related activities (guest lectures, presentations), and our suggestion to Marcus would be to highlight positive reviews of teaching (in terms of course evaluations by students and faculty members) and teaching-related contributions.

Search committee members will also check the candidate's references, which are usually in the form of letters of support from people who ostensibly are qualified to judge the applicant's abilities and character traits. Committee members' analyses of references are usually guided by a list of questions applied to each candidate for the available position. In the case of a position in a university, questions will include ones about both the individual's teaching and research experience and about her or his future potential in these areas. There will probably also be a question that aims to elicit comments about whether the applicant would be a positive, cooperative colleague.

Now a word about references. Determine your vocational goal as you identify whom to ask for a letter of support. Your academic advisor in graduate school and perhaps other faculty members usually serve as references. Perhaps you're working with someone who is well known in an area of research in which you would like to establish yourself. That is likely an excellent reference. You might ask potential letter writers if they feel they know you well enough to provide a suitable recommendation. This approach lets you know whether they will likely provide a supportive reference, and it also gives them a way out in case they feel that they cannot.

In summary, your written job application will be reviewed by a department head and probably by a search committee that will discuss, debate, and rate your apparent qualifications. If you are one of the more highly rated candidates, members of the committee will also contact your references and ask them a predetermined slate of questions, usually having to do with your teaching and research potential. Based on all of these ratings, the committee typically determines which slate of candidates will be invited to engage in phone or videoconference interviews. A series of interviews may be scheduled, for example at thirty-minute intervals with different committee members. Usually the committee chair will preside and department members will participate. They may have a list of identical questions that they ask each candidate.

HOW TO CREATE A STELLAR CV

As noted earlier, a curriculum vitae (CV) is a record of your professional history and qualifications. You need to send your CV when applying for a teaching position. The CV is something you'll continually develop and use throughout your academic life. You'll present it when applying for grants, when informing a book editor of your background as you submit a manuscript for publication, when you are being considered for a promotion, and when asked about your credentials by the person who introduces you as a guest lecturer or as an interviewee on a television or radio program.

What, then, should you include in your professional biography, and in what order should the information be arranged? Typical sections of CVs are ones that focus on (a) personal identification information, (b) educational background, (c) teaching experience, (d) research experience and interests, (e) practical experience related to one's field of academic expertise, (f) past employment relevant to the teaching position at hand, (g) publications and performances, (h) presentations at conferences, (i) membership in significant organizations, (j) awards and distinctions, (k) service, and (l) special skills and knowledge.

The sequence in which information is most effectively presented can depend on the type of job for which you are applying. If you are seeking a position in a two-year community college, it would be well to feature your teaching experience and interests early in the document, along with your relevant practical experience. Then leave any mention of research interests to later in the CV. In contrast, if you are applying for a tenure-track position in a university that highly values research, you would be wise to place your research section early in your CV—probably immediately after the teaching section—accompanied by your record of publications and presentations at highly regarded conferences.

The cover letter that you submit with your application can also highlight the aspects of your background that are most relevant to the nature of the job for which you are applying. We turn now to the typical sections into which CVs are organized.

Your personal identification information can properly include your full name, postal address, email address, phone number, and website (if you have one). Do not include personal information such as age, religion, children, or marital status.

The educational background section should list the post-secondary schools you have attended, the dates of attendance, and degrees or certificates earned.

The description of your teaching experience can include tutoring, small-group mentoring, and classroom instruction of all varieties, but with emphasis placed on situations that are closest to what you expect in the job you are seeking. For example, when you apply for a Spanish language lectureship, your having served as a teaching assistant for an Italian language professor will be of greater interest to members of a search committee than will your having taught water safety to juveniles in a summer camp.

Next is the research portion of your professional record. If you are seeking a position in a two-year community college or in a four-year liberal arts college that focuses primarily on teaching, your research record may be of little or no interest to search committees. However, evidence of your potential as a researcher and creator of new knowledge is critical if you are aiming at a tenure-track post in a college or university that is ambitious to increase its prestige as a font of scholarship. In such a school, not only will those who judge your potential be curious about the research you have already done (often in the form of your master's thesis or doctoral dissertation), but they will also like to know what matters you intend to investigate in the years ahead. Therefore, a brief description of research topics that you envision for the future could usefully be included in the CV.

The practical experience and past employment parts of your CV provide an opportunity to describe events in your past that should help you succeed as a teacher. Those experiences may have resulted from where you've lived, where you've traveled, organizations you've joined, people you've known, jobs you've held, and hobbies you've pursued.

As noted in chapter 4, skill at publishing, performing, and creating products is highly valued in four-year institutions. Such skill is often essential for long-term security of employment and promotion to higher ranks. Ostensibly, teaching and publishing are weighed equally in decisions about retaining and promoting faculty members. However, in the typical university, respectable publishing, performing, and product development trump teaching. This imbalance results partly from the difficulty of assessing the quality of a person's teaching. Students' ratings of their teachers may not be trustworthy, some professors are fine teachers for certain kinds of students but not for other kinds, and faculty members cannot directly assess colleagues' teaching effectiveness because they rarely visit each other's classes. In short, a teacher's performance is not open to public view—but not so with publications (journal articles, books) or performances (lectures, music recitals, theatrical productions), and products (art exhibits, computer programs). To make clear some nuances of publishing and performing that can affect the form and content of your CV, at this juncture we'll describe those aspects of university life in greater detail.

Respectable publishing in academia is usually in the form of articles in learned journals, of books issued by "reputable" publishers, and of chapters in other academics' books. An article written for a highly regarded encyclopedia could qualify as well. However, writing articles for newspapers and popular magazines, or paying to have your own book published, will usually get you nowhere with search committees. Of course, if a professor with a distinguished record pens an article that appears on the op-ed page of a newspaper, that act does not injure her reputation as a scholar, but neither does it add any luster to her academic record. Recognizing this, she will not add the article to her list of professional publications. So, if you have published in a newspaper, newsletter, or magazine, it's probably not worth listing in your CV.

When professors judge the quality of articles in academic journals, they often draw a distinction between peer-refereed (peer-reviewed) and non-refereed journals. A refereed journal is one in which each manuscript submitted to editors by an author is sent to two or three experts in the journal's field—atomic physics, German literature, art criticism, cultural anthropology, or the like. The experts serve as referees, assigned to judge the quality of the article and return their opinions to the editor. Manuscripts that fail to meet the referees' standards are rejected. The editor publishes only those articles approved by the referees. (Frequently an author is asked to make improvements in an article before it will be published.) In contrast to refereed journals are non-refereed periodicals in which editors make their own decisions about what to publish, free of any input from experts in the journal's subject-matter field. This does not mean that an article in a non-refereed journal is of less scholarly value than one in a peer-reviewed publication, but the likelihood is that articles in peer-refereed journals have been subjected to greater scholarly scrutiny. The significance of this situation for your CV is that when you list your publications, you should distinguish peer-reviewed from non-peer-reviewed items.

Usually new master's degree and doctoral graduates have few publications, but they are currently in the process of publishing, perhaps in the form of a journal article based on their recently completed thesis or maybe a book or monograph that is a concise version of their dissertation. If the work has been accepted by a publisher but is not yet in print, it can be listed in the CV as in press. (If you have some page proofs or sample chapters of your manuscript, you could send them for the committee's inspection.) Or perhaps your article hasn't been accepted for publication because you are still working on it. You can then list it as in progress or in preparation. However, citing works as in progress can do more harm than good if you have a lot of such publications, thereby causing search committee members to suspect that you have a host of "great ideas" in mind but you haven't really written any of them. Committee members may view you as a "big talker" but not much of a "doer." There are more than enough "big talkers" and "non-doers" already among faculty members. Department chairs and deans don't yearn for any more. Furthermore, search committees are not interested in people with good ideas but not the diligence to get those ideas published and earn tenure at their institution.

Next, consider your active participation in professional conferences. This portion of your CV can be particularly important because, as a recent graduate, you are likely to have made several conference presentations, even though your record of published research may be slim or nonexistent. You hope that your conference activity is interpreted by search committees as a harbinger of your future scholarly productivity. Your participation at conferences can take several forms. You may be a guest speaker, a presenter of a paper, an official responder to a presentation, a panel discussion member, a judge of papers submitted for presentation, or a conference organizer; which of these roles you played can be indicated on your CV. As in the case of publications, people who judge your suitability for a college teaching position may distinguish between refereed and non-refereed conferences. Refereed conferences are ones in which applicants who wish to present a paper must submit ahead of time their paper or an abstract of it. The conference sponsors inspect the submissions, judge their suitability, then include only the chosen ones on the conference program. In contrast, there is no such vetting system for non-refereed conferences. Either all submissions are accepted or else the program is filled on a first-come-first-served basis until all presentation spots are taken. Therefore you may wish to indicate on your CV which of the conferences in which you played an active part were refereed and which were not.

Furthermore, you may want to include a section on published conference proceedings, i.e., refereed conference proceedings (where submitted papers also go through a review process by two or three experts in the field, and if accepted, your paper goes through a revision process and is submitted to an editor, analogous to the refereed journal publication process). In different disciplines, refereed conference proceedings may be accorded varying degrees of regard. For example, a refereed conference paper presented at a prestigious computer science or educational technology conference would be valued highly (although not as highly in most cases as a refereed journal article) because these are fields where innovations and research need to be disseminated rapidly to keep abreast of new technologies. In such areas, the lag time between submitting an article to a journal and actual publication (sometimes as long as a year) might render some research quickly outdated. To find out how significant conference proceedings are in your discipline and how to include them on your CV, we recommend consulting with faculty members, and inspecting CV's of successful faculty members on the web.

We turn now to your membership in organizations. The principal groups to which you belong are probably the sorts of professional and academic societies described in chapter 4. If you hold an office, are on committees, or have special status (that of fellow, diplomate, patron) in an association, you should include that information in your CV. In addition, other types of associations may also be important to list—ones that can contribute to the quality of your teaching and research. Such is the case of an ornithologist who is active in the Audubon Society, an economist who is a member of Junior Chamber of Commerce, an agronomist who belongs to the Future Farmers of America Alumni Association, an English language major who is in the Science Fiction Writers Association, and a historian in the Swedish Ancestry Research Association.

The grants section of your CV can include financial grants that you have obtained, and your role (PI or Principal Investigator, or co-PI). You should also list the amount and funding source.

The awards-and-distinctions section of your professional biography can include such accomplishments as scholarships, fellowships, awards for papers you published, distinguished-scholar citations, the role of valedictorian or salutatorian, and the like.

The CV's service section concerns one of the three principal criteria used in most colleges for judging faculty members when they are being considered for retention or promotion. As explained in chapter 3, the two most important criteria concern (a) teaching and (b) research and creative activity. The third standard—service—is regarded as important, but in decisions about whether to hire, retain, or promote a faculty member, a strong service record cannot compensate for weak teaching and/or weak research. Excellent teaching and, especially, a stellar research and performance record can lead to promotion even when the service record is poor or nonexistent. What, then, is meant by service? The focus of the service requirement can be any or all of three venues—one's college or university (especially one's academic department), one's academic discipline or profession (psychology, sports medicine, literary criticism, religious studies, and the like), and one's community (local, state, and/or nation). When institutions advertise teaching positions, they often include in the job description such phrases as "department or university service, and professionally related service are expected," "required to participate in university/college/department and professional activities," and "assigned to provide service to the university and the community." What, then, might you include on your CV to suggest that you would be a willing and efficient servant if hired in the position for which you are applying? To identify examples that you might cite, recall jobs you've held in the past, charitable organizations you've aided, and schools you've attended. In particular, consider your years in graduate school. Were you a teaching assistant, a research assistant, a voluntary aide to a professor or a group; if so, what did you do that could be interpreted as service to the college? Were you a member of a committee, a tutor, or an officer in a student organization? At the local city or state level, did you contribute to community improvement events or charity drives? In the field of your academic specialization, did you serve on local, state, or national committees? Reporting such activities on your CV can suggest to search committee members that you would fulfill the service expectations held for their faculty members.

Finally, you may wish to add information about special skills and knowledge that you would bring to the institution that hires you. Having a breadth of knowledge is one form of special ability. Having unusually detailed knowledge of highly specialized variety is another form. Thus, either breadth of knowledge and depth of knowledge can be an advantage in job hunting. First, consider breadth of knowledge. Imagine that you are applying for a teaching position in a university's school of education. In graduate school, you had majored in language arts curricula and methods, but you had also minored in social studies curricula and methods. Therefore, you are qualified to offer instruction and to conduct research in both of those fields. That can save the college from needing to hire two professors to cover the two fields. Or you are a candidate for a political science position, and you can read, speak, and write English, Russian, Arabic, and Farsi, thereby equipping you to study the political science literature in all four tongues and to communicate with native speakers of each language. Second, consider depth of knowledge. Imagine that you are applying for a job in a sociology department. During your graduate studies, you developed an unusually sophisticated knowledge of sampling procedures in survey research. Because so much sociological research involves surveys, the ability to create and critique sampling methods and put them into practice is highly prized. If you were hired, you could be a valuable aid to your colleagues and students. Or assume that you are an astronomer who has specialized in building radio telescopes and interpreting the results of observations. Such expertise could be a boon to a college's science department.

In summary, taking care in composing your professional history in the form of a curriculum vitae can determine whether you are considered by a research committee to be a promising candidate for a college post.

HOW TO SHINE DURING A TELEPHONE INTERVIEW

How can you make yourself stand out at the telephone interview level? The suggestions below about what to do (and not to do) have emerged from our having participated as search committee members in numerous phone interviews. As a job-seeking candidate, you will be wise to:

- Select a time and place for the interview that is quiet and where you'll not be interrupted by music, family members arguing, or colleagues talking.

- Make sure in advance that your technology — the phone connection, the video — is working properly. Test it out with one of your friends.
- Be available at lease 15 minutes before the scheduled interview. Be prepared to have technology backups. For example, if it's a videoconference via an Internet telephone program, make sure you have provided the search committee your cell number or another phone number at which you can be reached, as a backup.
- Recognize that if you aren't called exactly at the scheduled time, it's possible that the search committee could still be talking to the previous candidate, or perhaps having technical difficulties of its own. Be patient.
- Have paper and pencil with you. When interviewers introduce themselves, write down their names and any quick relevant notes.
- You might write down questions or a few keywords as interviewers ask questions, using the key words to prompt yourself as you answer.
- Ask for clarification. That is, don't be afraid to ask for questions to be repeated, or to request a moment to think about your answer.
- Do your homework in advance of the phone interview! Find out ahead of time about the department, university, faculty members' research interests and specializations. The more you know about the nature of the department, the university, and its faculty, the more seriously interested in the position you appear. Search committee members are impressed with candidates who have done their homework, read members' articles, and know about their university. The more you know about the social, cultural, and academic milieu you're being considered for, the more likely you might be a good candidate, and be someone who would be satisfied to teach at the institution. In contrast, the less you know, and the less you appear seriously interested in the institution, the less likely you will favorably impress the committee.
- Be aware of time. You might even ask if there is a certain amount of time to be allocated for the interview. This allows you to better gauge how much time to allocate to answering a question.
- Be aware of normal conversational give and take. If you've been talking for an extended amount of time with no time for the interviewer to respond, you won't know if the interviewer has been

raptly listening or bored. The phone interview tells not only your literal answers to questions but a bit about your interactive and teaching style. So be to-the-point! You might even practice answering questions that you might be expected to be asked, such as about your teaching style or instructional experiences, or your research area.

- Realize that there will probably be a point at the end where you will be asked if you have any questions. At this juncture, it would likely be an error to ask basic questions about the university (How many students?) or department (What kinds of courses do you offer?) that you could easily have found the answers to by a simple Internet search! Here are some more acceptable kinds of final questions: What is the regular teaching load? Is there a reduced teaching load for new faculty members? Are there research expectations? Will a laboratory or start-up funds for research be provided? Are there teaching reductions for new faculty members? What is the next step in the search process? But don't drag out this part of the interview just to keep talking.
- Thank the committee members at the end.

INTERVIEWING AT CONFERENCES

Another productive choice for higher education job seekers is to interview at national or regional conferences. Many larger professional associations in various disciplines have interview services or employment websites at which you can register.

Typically, you post a shortened CV to a website potential employers can search, and you can look at jobs that are compiled in a listing, or sign up to be emailed job announcements that meet certain criteria that you set, such as your academic field and geographic region in which you hope to work. If you see a position that interests you, apply for it. You also may be contacted by potential employers that are interested in interviewing you. Interviews actually take place on-site at the conference in booths set up for that purpose.

The first author of this book, when she was still a graduate student, found that conference interviews were excellent ways to make connections for future employment. In fact she signed up to interview before most candidates would be thinking about interviewing—that is, before she started her dissertation. Her goal was to find out what the interview process was like and see what kinds of positions were available. She found that it was best to be open to a broader range of possible jobs than she would have selected for herself, because employers from slightly different fields found aspects of her expertise that meshed with their employment needs. She kept in contact with one department chair who wanted to be apprised of her dissertation progress, and another employer suggested that although her area did not exactly match the qualifications for the position for which they were hiring, he could find out whether other positions would be available. She found that interviewing at a conference was much more useful for her than applying for positions via mail only.

This kind of networking is also invaluable from the employer's side. It is, of course, less expensive to interview five to ten candidates face-to-face, and perhaps see their conference presentations, than it is to invite two or three people out for interviews at the employer's own college. If candidates seem especially promising, they might be invited to meet other faculty members who are present at the conference. Or candidates might create the kind of network that will serve them well for future employment opportunities.

HOW TO ACE YOUR ON-SITE INTERVIEWS

If the quality of your CV, telephone interview, or conference interview convince the search committee that you are good prospect for the position they are trying to fill, you likely will be invited to visit the college campus. By being invited for an on-site interview, you are apt to be one of the few top candidates being considered for the position, so you have a good chance of getting the job. But if you are not invited shortly after your telephone interview, should you give up in despair? Probably not, because the search committee may be inviting other candidates to visit the campus before you. A bit of patience is needed.

When you arrive on campus, you can typically expect the following events:

- An initial interview with the dean or division director.
- An interview with the department chairperson.
- Interviews with individual faculty members.
- A meeting with graduate students as a group.

- Meetings with other key faculty members or constituents, such as faculty members or groups outside the department with whom you would be expected to collaborate when you were a member of the faculty.
- Luncheon or dinner with the department as a group.
- Your presenting a "job talk."
- A final interview with the dean or department head.

What errors you can profitably avoid committing during your visit? The following are a few of the more obvious faux pas:

Wearing unprofessional attire. If you dress like the vision of a serious professor, it's an indication that you take the interview seriously. Appropriate attire includes proper business attire, such as a suit or dress and business shoes. If you notice that some of the people who interview you are dressed very casually, don't imagine that you should emulate them—at least, not until after you are hired. So, decide the level of professionalism you want to convey and dress accordingly. If you are confused about what's best, err on the more professional side.

Confiding inappropriate information. The people interviewing you are doing a job. They likely will be friendly, but you should not think of them as your friends and then confide inappropriate information, ask personal questions about other faculty members and their relationships, or ask about other candidates who applying for the job you seek, even if you already know someone on the search committee or you find certain faculty members especially compatible.

Wasting people's time. The faculty members who spend hours with you are busy people, so it is wise to be considerate of their time. Before your visit, you might ask for a schedule to be emailed to you, so you get an idea of how much time is allocated for each event.

Failing to show interest in the people you meet. Most faculty members will be pleased to learn that you are interested in their work. Thus, if you learn ahead of time the names of interviewers you will meet, you can search the Internet to find information about their academic specialties and accomplishments—perhaps their research and teaching interests. That information can help guide your conversation when you meet them.

Failing to show appreciation. You will make a better impression if you sincerely thank the people you meet for the time they have spent with you.

Most campus visits last two days. However, you may wish to extend the time for an extra day so you can learn more about the community in which the college is set, particularly about the types and costs of housing, the area's cultural attractions, public safety, and schools.

How to Impress with Your Job Talk

Among the tasks you are likely to be asked to perform during your visit to the campus of your potential employer is that of giving a formal presentation to a group. This job talk is expected to illustrate how you might give a lecture or demonstration to a class you would teach. The audience for your job talk will probably include faculty members (particularly ones from the search committee), administrators (dean, department head), and students. The subject matter of your talk will be something in your field of specialization, often focusing on the research for your dissertation. The audience is interested in observing (a) the scholarly quality of your thought processes, (b) how easy it is to follow your sequence of ideas, (c) how clearly you speak, (d) your grammar and choice of words, (e) how precisely you define your key terms, (f) what technologies you adopt to clarify what you mean, (g) whether you have mannerisms that distract from the effectiveness of your presentation, (h) how convincingly you answer questions, and the like.

At the time that you were originally invited to the campus, you probably were informed that you would be expected to give such a presentation. At that point it would have been wise for you to inquire about the details of the expected job talk, such as (a) what sorts of people would be in the audience, (b) what kind of topic they would like you to speak about, (c) how much time the session should take, and (d) the available room and technology facilities. Armed with this information, you prepare your talk and then practice the presentation before you go to the campus.

Here is an illustrative way to prepare. You choose to focus the talk on research you have either completed or are currently conducting. Such a talk is typically expected to last about an hour, including both the time for the presentation itself and subsequent discussion and questions. To help the audience follow your line of reasoning, you plan to accompany the talk with two sorts of visual aids—a presentation enhanced by the use of presentation software, such as Powerpoint and paper handouts containing diagrams tracing the sequence of ideas you present. (To guard against losing the Powerpoint presentation and handouts, you e-mail copies of them to a friend and to yourself so you could access them on someone else's computer when you reached the campus. Make sure you have handouts and a back-up plan if the technology fails.) If you are not accustomed to giving such presentations, you can improve your confidence level and the fluency of your presentation by practicing ahead of time, perhaps in front of several audiences of a few graduate students or professors and asking for their feedback. Such experience can help you adjust your timing so that you allow for questions at the end, you are not stumped by unexpected questions, and—if you don't know the answers—you are prompt to admit it and will be searching out the answer. In such practice sessions, you can have your performance videotaped so you can see how to improve. One way to learn to maintain your focus despite distractions is to practice in a noisy environment, perhaps with a television program playing at the time.

AFTER THE INTERVIEW

It's fitting to thank members of the interview committee for hosting you during the interview. A quick email to each person who played a major role in interviewing or hosting you would be appropriate. It's also appropriate to inquire about when a decision would likely be made about whom to offer the job. That inquiry would most profitably go to the search committee chair or department chair while you are on-site or shortly after.

The whole process of interviewing candidates can take up to several weeks, assuming that in most searches two or three candidates are invited out for interviews, and one candidate is interviewed per week. In addition to time interviewing, departments need to meet to discuss whether to recommend to the administration (usually the dean) that an offer be made and to whom. Such an offer will typically come from the dean's office, and it may take awhile to be negotiated with busy administrators. However, most departments are motivated to act quickly, knowing that strong candidates are likely interviewing elsewhere and might be receiving other offers. An offer might be made to a candidate who will be given a certain amount of time (perhaps a few days or a week) to make a decision. If that candidate turns down the position, the committee may have to meet again to determine whether an offer should be made to Candidate 2, and so on.

We mention these factors because we know that you are understandably impatient to learn about whether you have an offer or not. An inquiry about the status of the search might be appropriate a couple of weeks after the interview, but please remember that you do not want to appear to be hounding the committee chair, or worse yet, bothering committee members or administrators. You might also wonder if it is appropriate to mention that you have already received another offer, or to use the offer to leverage the position at your preferred institution. If you do have an offer and are under time pressure to make a decision, this would be important and fitting for the department to know. If you do not actually have an offer but pretend you do, such an approach could easily backfire, as you could be advised to accept that offer.

CONCLUSION

The intent of this chapter has been to sketch principal steps in the process of hunting for a teaching position in a higher education institution, particularly for a position on the tenure track of a four-year college or university, including institutions that offer graduate degrees. The seven steps have concerned (a) search committees' activities, (b) candidates creating their professional biographies in the form of curriculum vitae, (c) the conduct of telephone interviews, (d) opportunities for interviews at national and regional conferences, (e) being invited to visit the campus of a potential teaching position, (f) presenting a talk before an audience during a visit to the campus, and (g) what happens after the interview.

II

On-the-Job: Research/Creativity, Teaching, and Service Roles

Teachers in higher education institutions are typically expected to provide skillful instruction for students, to display creativity, and to serve needs of their institution, their profession, and their community. Part I of this book described the kinds of institutions and available positions in higher education, and provided tips for preparing oneself to successfully land a higher education position. Part II describes three roles that faculty member should be prepared to assume—the creativity (research), teaching, and service roles.

All professors are expected to be creative, and in most universities where there is a research expectation, faculty members are expected to display creativity in their published writings, their performances, and their products. Even in many colleges that have been traditionally focused on teaching, it is no longer enough for a faculty member to only be a creative teacher. It is also necessary to display creativity in some more publicly available form. Chapter 6 ("Publishing, Performing, and Products") offers a detailed analysis of three such forms.

Teaching is central to most faculty positions, although some higher education institutions, such as community colleges, might have a higher teaching expectation, with faculty teaching more courses than at other more research-oriented institutions. As we mentioned previously, we believe the teaching role to be so essential that we have written a separate book about teaching, *A Guide to Teaching in Colleges and Universities* (Iding and Thomas, in press). Chapter 7 ("Teaching") provides suggestions for beginning teachers about negotiating teaching loads, planning a course, and improving one's teaching.

Chapter 8 ("Service Obligations") focuses on ways that professors are expected to help in operating their college or university, in promoting the success of their academic specialization beyond their own campus, and in contributing to the welfare of the community in which their campus is located.

SIX

Publishing, Performing, and Products

As explained in chapters 4 and 5, the tasks of publishing scholarly writings, performing in academically respected venues, and creating valued products are essential for success in most tenure-track teaching positions. Although such activities are not required for survival in lectureships, instructorships, and adjunct professorships—or in colleges that focus almost exclusively on teaching—research and creative activities still add luster to faculty members' records, thereby bolstering job security, mobility, and hastening promotion to higher rank and pay.

The purpose of this chapter is to (a) describe types of publishing, performance, and products, (b) compare their advantages and disadvantages, and (c) identify ways to cope with common problems encountered during attempts to publish, perform, and display products.

At the outset, it is important to identify the meanings assigned to publishing, performing, and products. Publishing refers to a faculty member's writings being issued in print available to a reading audience, particularly in the form of books and of articles in academic journals. Performing means appearing before an audience to deliver a speech, play a musical instrument, act in a theatrical production, or the like. Products are observable items (other than print and electronic publications) that faculty members create, such as scientific instruments, oil paintings, architectural structures, or computer programs.

The chapter closes with suggestions about how faculty members can find the time needed to pursue research and creative activity in addition to their teaching and service responsibilities.

PUBLISHING

The issues addressed in the following paragraphs concern (a) types of media in which you can publish your contributions to knowledge, (b) kinds of content for your publications, and the relative merit of different kinds, (c) ways to submit manuscripts to editors, and (d) questions of quantity and quality of publications.

Types of Publishing Media

As a faculty member, you can publish your professional writings in various media, such as a:

- printed book, funded by a publisher
- chapter in someone else's printed book
- article in a printed or electronic scholarly journal
- electronic book (e-book)
- paper you gave at a conference that is then printed in a collection of conference proceedings
- encyclopedia article
- brochure
- article in a popular magazine
- newspaper article, such as an op-ed (editorial page) contribution

Not all types of media are judged of equal worth for purposes of advancement in higher education.

Books

Authoring a book is generally regarded as requiring greater effort and is assumed to be a greater contribution to knowledge than an article of similar quality in an academic journal. A book that you have written alone—or, is coauthored, with you listed as the senior (first) author—will usually earn more credit than a volume for which you are one of several coauthors. A chapter you wrote in someone else's book is likely to gain you the same credit as an article you wrote in an academic journal. A book issued by a "respected academic publisher" is valued above one issued by a "nondescript" or "popular fiction" publishing house. Higher education institutions often include a university press, a publishing facility that specializes in academic books, often for particular fields of knowledge. Such presses are usually well regarded in college circles because their editors take care to select only manuscripts that have passed the approval of experts in the field. Other "respected" publishing houses are ones known for issuing books by acclaimed scholars, so a volume from such a press can, in the minds of faculty promotion committees, bask in the reflected glory of those houses' reputations.

Some professors pay to have their book issued by what is known as a vanity press or vanity publisher or self-publish a book. Such practices afford an author greater liberty in determining the content of the book, because there usually is no vetting of the quality of the manuscript by academicians. But vanity press or self-publishing is risky business because there is the suspicion that the manuscript was not good enough to convince a regular publisher to take it on. This does not necessarily mean that a vanity press book is of poor quality. For example, a professor may be introducing a new theory that is in conflict with the conventional wisdom in his discipline. Thus, academicians who review manuscripts for traditional publishers may so disagree with the novel theory, which is not in keeping with their own beliefs, that they recommend to the editor that the manuscript be rejected. Or, the editor in a "respected" publishing house may believe such a book—despite its high quality—would have so few buyers that it would be a money loser. Hence, the manuscript is turned down for economic, rather than scholarly, reasons. Nowadays, with print publishers facing so much competition for readers from the Internet, recent years have witnessed increasing reluctance of academic publishers to accept manuscripts that they would have welcomed a decade or two ago. Thus, more professors may be obliged to finance—at least partially—tomes they pen. However, because self-published books do not need to pass a reviewing process by experts, such publications are not accorded the respect in academia that vetted books receive.

Journal Articles

In terms of prestige, publishing articles in academic journals is nearly equal to that of publishing a well-regarded book. However, as noted in chapter 5, a distinction is usually drawn by academicians between refereed and non-refereed journals. A refereed or reviewed journal is one in which a manuscript submitted to a journal is sent to two or three experts in the particular field of knowledge. The experts judge the worth of the manuscript and advise the editor about whether the work is of acceptable quality and should be published, or what changes would need to be made to render it acceptable. A non-refereed journal is one in which the editor decides whether to publish a manuscript, with no advice from scholars in the field. Faculty members who are judging their colleagues' publications usually rate refereed articles over non-refereed ones. Although publishing in a refereed journal does not guarantee that the article is a significant contribution to knowledge, or that a piece in a non-refereed periodical is insignificant, the chances are that manuscripts that have passed the scrutiny of scholars are of greater worth than ones that have not. It is also the case that journals vary in their acceptance rates, so that some journals accept a smaller percentage of submissions than do others. Consequently a manuscript may be quite worthy, but not as important as others in the opinion of editors. Thus, an article that is rejected by a journal that prints only 25 percent of submissions might be accepted by one that publishes 50 percent of submissions. In some cases you might have to document acceptance rates of journals as part of your application for tenure or promotion, so a journal with a lower acceptance rate of 10 percent or less would usually be considered more prestigious than a journal with an acceptance rate of 50 percent.

Another type of metric that can show the influence of a publication is citation impact. Thus, an article in a prestigious journal that is cited by numerous researchers afterward would have a higher citation impact. These are calculated by various means, so you might find out whether they are useful for you to use at your particular institution and in your department.

Electronic Publications and Blogs

The term electronic publishing refers mainly to books and articles disseminated via the Internet. Electronic publishing enjoys a variety of obvious advantages over traditional print publishing (books, journals, magazines on paper). Compared to print publishing, it is much faster, less expensive, available to a far broader audience, more conveniently stored, and ecologically more friendly.

In print publishing, the time gap between (a) an editor accepting a finished book manuscript and (b) the book being published is typically a year or more. For a quarterly academic journal in print, the gap is as short as several months or as long as two years or more. In contrast, the time gap with electronic publishing can be as brief as a few days or few weeks if the manuscript needs little or no editing.

The cost of producing traditional books and journals has been high. It involves expensive typesetting, printing, advertising, and distributing. Although e-publishing involves computer typesetting, the task does not require a highly paid professional typesetter. There are no printing costs, no problems of distributing books to booksellers, no mailing costs for journals sent to subscribers, and no unsold books and journals in storage facilities.

All scholarly journals that we currently use have online versions, available through university libraries. And most major scholarly books are disseminated in electronic versions as well. Thus, it is apparent that e-publishing is overtaking print publishing as the chief outlet for disseminating scholarly work. However, some major questions are associated with e-publishing, and in this section we address several of the most important ones.

An initial question is about the scholarly value of electronic journals. We note that over the past several years, numerous new electronic journals have appeared and disseminated mass emails requesting submissions—an uncommon if not nonexistent practice among well-regarded scholarly outlets. For example, in an article entitled, "Scientific Articles Accepted (Personal Checks, Too)," *New York Times* writer Kolata (2013) explored the "parallel world of pseudo-academia, complete with prestigiously titled conferences and journals that sponsor them . . . [with] names that are nearly identical to those of established, well-known publications and events" (para. 4). Well-intentioned academics described themselves as feeling "duped" after succumbing to emailed solicitations to submit manuscripts, present at conferences, or serve on review boards. Kolata quotes Steven Goodman, professor of medicine and dean at Stanford who refers to this as the "dark side of open access" (para. 6). Since these conferences and journals can be quite profitable (much to the surprise of naïve authors and presenters when they receive invoices to publish their work), we see no end to this kind of practice in the near future and we urge caution. It is best to publish in known, reputable scientific outlets that well-established colleagues in your field publish in and are knowledgeable about. Furthermore, your colleagues may be happy to give some scholarly advice to you if you have questions about particular outlets.

What about electronic scholarship generally? Here we rely on the wise words of Davidson (2008) who explains:

> Excellent scholarship should not be excluded from a tenure file simply because the form of its production happens to be electronic. If the scholarship is refereed by scholars in the field and deemed publishable, if it has impact and meets the highest professional standards, it is hard to think of what possible, rational argument could be made against it counting in the way its equivalent paper-version would count. Scientists often publish in journals that exist only on line. We have plenty of models out there that have been accepted in a range of disciplines where no one has problems distinguishing "excellent" from "okay" scholarship simply because its mode of production happens to be electronic. (para. 4)

Davidson (2008) further points out that what is determined to be scholarship will be determined by one's department and one's university. Thus, the ultimate arbiters of whether something "counts" for tenure are those who are tenured, and who have become so inside the system. In her words:

> "Counting for tenure" needs some serious deconstructing. One version of that sentence sometimes translates as: "I didn't do what I was supposed to do according to all the documents about tenure I've been reading for the past six years. I did something else. Now I'm up for tenure. And I'm worried." There is reason to be worried. It's almost impossible to change the rules for tenure at the same time that you yourself are up for tenure—at least not by yourself! (para. 6–7)

As Davidson advises (2010), the system of peer review is what is central to the tenure and promotion process in academia, and so she also addresses the question (in her blog, of course) about whether a blog should "count" for such decisions. She says "yes" but not as scholarship. Instead, it should count as service because it has not gone through a peer review process: "Precisely what I love about blogs and about blogging myself is that it is not refereed. I write what I want and people can choose to read or not" (Davidson, 2010, para 4).

There are probably many other forms of digital scholarship that will emerge and which we can only imagine at the time of this writing, such as contributions to history, cultural studies, and the arts. However, the process of peer review will likely remain central to academic scholarship for the foreseeable future, so we recommend selecting outlets for your research and creative works that have strong foundations in recognized peer review structures—and structures that are clearly valued at your institution.

Published Conference Presentations

Frequently the papers presented at scholarly conferences are published, either as abstracts or as a collection of writings relating to a conference theme. Consequently, such a paper is available in printed form to reading audiences so the quality of your thinking process can be judged. For promotion committee members, such detailed evidence is more useful than simply a conference presentation's title. But because in some disciplines contributions to conferences often have not been screened for quality—that is, they are not "refereed"—people who judge your work may not attach as much importance to published proceedings as they would to a journal article or chapter in a book.

However, highly regarded conferences are usually refereed—that is, you submit your conference proposal—an abstract or paper (with identifying information removed)—and anonymous referees review it to determine if it is acceptable. Such conferences can also provide you with statistics that indicate acceptance rates. If you are uncertain about a conference's value or ranking, you might consult with your faculty advisor from your graduate program or other faculty members in your department. If a conference is not considered refereed, that is, proposals are accepted outright without a scholarly review process, it will probably not be considered as a scholarly contribution for tenure and promotion purposes.

Further, for some conferences (such as in computer science or other technology-related fields where technical innovations and related research are rapidly disseminated), you may have the additional opportunity to publish a refereed conference paper. Thus, your contribution goes through two levels of review—an initial level that determines whether your conference proposal is accepted for presentation—and a secondary level where the paper is reviewed by anonymous reviewers (as is the case with regular journal publications) and a determination of whether the paper merits publication is made and suggestions for revision are made. In addition to completing revisions, you will usually have to format your paper in some precise camera-ready layout. Although such a publication has scholarly merit (and the extent to which it does depends on your field, the reputation of the conference, and your department's determinations of its value), it typically does not have the same value as a publication in a refereed journal.

Conferences frequently also offer participants a semi-publishing opportunity—a poster presentation—that can serve as the entry-level method for graduate students and young professors to distribute the results of their scholarship. Here is a typical description of a conference poster presentation.

> A poster session is a graphic presentation of authors' reports. The authors illustrate their findings by displaying graphs, photos, diagrams and a small amount of text on the poster boards. . . . Authors will then hold discussions with the registrants who are circulating among the poster boards. Many authors find it helpful to present a brief introduction to answer the obvious questions and allow the remainder of the time for more in-depth discussions. . . . The author must remain by his/her poster board for the duration of the one hour session. . . . If handouts are distributed, bring approximately fifty copies. (American Public Health Association, 2014)

Finally, conferences are valuable for disseminating your work, making professional contacts with others, and learning about the latest innovations in your research area. At most universities there are opportunities to apply for travel funds to cover all or some of your expenses, and often the work of new professors is prioritized for funding, so you would be well advised to inquire about these opportunities with your department chairperson.

Encyclopedia Articles

Until the advent of the Internet, readers consulted encyclopedias to find trustworthy summaries of knowledge about the world. Encyclopedias have been of various kinds. General encyclopedias like the *Britannica, Americana,* and *World Book* offer concise accounts of all sorts of matters from all historical eras. Specialized encyclopedias furnish more detailed information about particular fields of knowledge or particular eras—

Encyclopedia of Educational Research, Encyclopedia of Human Development, International Encyclopedia of the Social and Behavioral Sciences, Encyclopedia of Science and Technology, and *Oxford Encyclopedia of the Modern World.*

As encyclopedia editors seek authors of articles, they attempt to find individuals regarded as experts in their specialized fields of knowledge. As a result, most encyclopedia entries are written by college professors, whose academic affiliations appear in the encyclopedia's list of contributors.

How, then, might the worth of an article you wrote for an encyclopedia be judged by your colleagues? It would count in your favor, but that article—or even several such entries—would not be sufficient to guarantee appointment or promotion to a tenure-track position. You would need, in addition, a substantial set of journal articles or a well-regarded book.

Other Media

Some college professors write outside the mainstream of academic publications, including articles in popular magazines, newspapers, and newsletters, political or commercial brochures, and testimonials for products or charities. In addition, some write novels, children's books, cookbooks, travel leaflets, book reviews, and similar works. Listing such contributions on your professional curriculum vitae will likely do no harm, so long as you also have a solid record of publishing in your field of knowledge. In effect, reviewers of your record may think such pastime publishing is "interesting"—such as Albert Einstein's playing the violin—but of no value for supporting your scholarly worth. If you do not have a substantial record of what might be called hardcore academic publishing, then including other media contributions will likely make you appear a bit desperate.

KINDS OF PUBLISHING CONTENT

The content of what you publish can vary markedly, with some kinds of content carrying greater value in academia than other kinds. And the worth of different kinds can vary from one scholarly discipline or college department to another. The following discussion is designed to illustrate such distinctions by offering a sample of different sorts of content and by speculating about how those sorts are valued by faculty members and administrators who make decisions about the appointment and promotion of professors. The kinds of content described below are not intended to form a definitive survey of published material. Instead, they represent only five samples of the wide variety of content in academic publications. The five are theories, textbooks, histories, biographies, and book reviews.

Theories

The word *theory* is used here to identify a proposal about the cause of some phenomenon. In the field of astrophysics, the big bang theory is a proposal about what caused the physical universe. In biology, Charles Darwin's theory is an estimate of how life forms originate. In psychology, Sigmund Freud's theory is an explanation of what causes neuroses. In linguistics, Noam Chomsky's theory of formal grammar is an attempt to account for the productivity or creativity of language.

Typically, a theory consists of a scholar identifying a limited number of variables and suggesting how the interaction of those variables causes the phenomenon of interest. In academia, creating a convincing theory is highly valued, as suggested by the fame of such individuals as Nicolaus Copernicus, Albert Einstein, Marie Curie, Karl Marx, and John Maynard Keynes. As a faculty member, you can earn credit in the realm of theory by creating a new one, convincingly critiquing an existing one, extending someone else's theory, illustrating the application of a theory to life situations, or explaining in simpler language a highly complex theory. Among these five sorts of contributions, the ones earlier in our list will likely win you greater credit than the later ones.

All academic disciplines or departments esteem contributions to theory—the physical sciences, social sciences, humanities, arts, and such applied fields as engineering, education, and social work.

Textbooks

A textbook is a compilation of knowledge in a field or subject, cast in a form that can be readily understood by students. The book can either summarize knowledge in a domain (European history, quantum physics, urban sociology, theories of learning) or be designed to teach a skill (architectural drawing, playing the harp, ceramic creations, computer programming). The content of textbooks describing a scholarly domain are in the form of secondary sources and tertiary sources rather than primary sources.

The following is a typical distinction among primary, secondary, and tertiary sources, from the University of Maryland Libraries (2014):

Primary sources are original materials. They are from the time period involved and have not been filtered through interpretation or evaluation. . . . They present original thinking, report a discovery, or share new information. . . . Examples include:

- Artifacts (e.g., coins, plant specimens, fossils, furniture, tools, clothing, all from the time under study)
- Audio recordings (e.g., radio programs)
- Diaries
- Internet communications on email, listservs
- Interviews (e.g., oral histories, telephone, e-mail)
- Journal articles published in peer-reviewed publications
- Original documents
- Survey research
- Video recordings

Secondary sources . . . generally are accounts written after the fact with the benefit of hindsight. They are interpretations and evaluations of primary sources. Secondary sources are not evidence, but rather are commentary on and discussion of evidence. . . . Examples include:

- Bibliographies
- Biographical works
- Commentaries, criticisms
- Dictionaries, Encyclopedias
- Histories
- Journal articles (depending on the discipline, can be primary)
- Magazine and newspaper articles (this distinction varies by discipline)
- Monographs, other than fiction and autobiography
- Textbooks (also considered tertiary)
- Website (also considered primary)

Tertiary sources consist of information which is a distillation and collection of primary and secondary sources:

- Almanacs
- Bibliographies (also considered secondary)

- Chronologies
- Dictionaries and encyclopedias (also considered secondary)
- Directories
- Fact books
- Guidebooks
- Indexes, abstracts, bibliographies used to locate primary and secondary sources
- Manuals
- Textbooks (also considered secondary)

Textbooks that you write will count to your credit in tenure and promotion decisions. However, a textbook usually will not be regarded as important as a noteworthy academic book or journal article that represents a primary source, unless your textbook displays particularly penetrating insight or a novel interpretive framework. The term framework here means the overall plan or structure of the text that serves as a new lens through which to view the volume's subject matter.

Histories

Accounts of the past, along with their insightful interpretation, are honored in all scholarly disciplines. However, writing history (in book or article form) is usually accorded greatest respect in history departments, since chronicling and interpreting the past is the core task of history department faculty members. However, merely telling a tale that has been told before without adding new source data or an innovative, convincing interpretation will not be regarded as much of a contribution to the field and will not likely win tenure or a promotion.

Outside of history departments, other types of contributions will often rank higher on the prestige scale than a historical account. In the computer science field, creating a novel computer program will be accorded greater credit than will a history of computing. In the music department, a widely acclaimed symphony composition will trump a history of organ music. In the anthropology department, an account of tribal life in very remote Amazon village will likely be considered more important than another history of Bronisław Malinowski's adventures in the South Pacific.

Biographies

Like histories, the significance of biographies varies by disciplines. Particularly in language and literature departments (Greek, Latin, English, French, Spanish, German, Slavic, and all the rest) biographies are most faculty members' principal publications. Scholars frequently base their careers on their expertise in the writings of a particular author—Shakespeare, Goethe, Dickens, Cervantes, Steinbeck, Pasternak, Voltaire. Or they specialize in a literary period or style—the British romantic period, French postmodernism, the Yuan dynasty. Likewise, in a philosophy department, specializing in the writings of Aristotle, Thomas Aquinas, Kant, or Dewey can constitute a successful academic career.

In disciplines outside of language and literature departments, biographies of important personages in the discipline are valued, but usually not so highly regarded as other sorts of contributions—reports of the inner workings of a political campaign by a political science professor, the discovery of a new galaxy by an astronomer, or the invention of a low cost and highly potent solar energy panel in an engineering department.

Book Reviews

The notion that reviewing books is a thriving business is suggested by the fact that *Book Review Digest Plus* provides citations to over 2 million book reviews. College professors are often the authors of reviews.

It is useful to recognize the difference between a review and a critique.

> The simplest criterion for distinguishing book reviews from literary criticism is the time of publication of the review/critical article compared to the original publication date of the book. Book reviews are written around the time the book was originally published; literary criticism appears in later years. For example, reviews of F. Scott Fitzgerald's *The Great Gatsby* that appeared in 1925 or 1926 (right after the novel was published) are book reviews, while literary criticism about the novel continues to be written today. (Cornell University Libraries, 2013)

Book reviews that you include in your list of professional publications will usually be ones in scholarly journals rather than in popular magazines, newspapers, or newsletters. When you contemplate writing a review, it is important to recognize that only a limited number of journals in your field of expertise include book reviews. For instance, for each of the following ten fields we have identified two journals that do publish book reviews.

- Anthropology—*American Anthropologist, Cultural Anthropology*
- Biology—*Journal of Plant Physiology, Biochemistry and Molecular Biology Education*
- Computer Science—*Computer Science Review, Journal of Intelligent Information Systems*
- Economics—*World Economics, Journal of Economic Literature*
- Education—*International Review of Education, Education Review*
- Geology—*Journal of Applied Earth Observations and Geoinformation, Journal of Geology*
- Literature and languages—*Modern Language Journal, Modern Language Review*
- Physics—*Contemporary Physics, International Journal of Theoretical Physics*
- Psychology—*Contemporary Psychology, American Journal of Psychology*
- Sociology—*Social Forces, American Journal of Sociology*

How important, then, are book reviews and critiques for your progress toward tenure and for promotion in rank and salary? The answer can depend on the review's academic discipline, the nature of the review, where the review is published and departmental criteria that might specify the value of reviews.

Reviews—and particularly ones in the form of literary criticism—will usually be considered of greater import in literature and language departments than in many other disciplines, because writing critiques is the principal business of so many literature and language faculty members.

By the phrase nature of the review, we mean how insightful and unique your review appears in the eyes of your colleagues who are involved in tenure and promotion decisions. A review that merely summarizes the content of a book is considered of less value than one that offers readers a convincing perspective from which to understand the book. Furthermore, a review published in a highly selective, prestigious journal will probably be accorded greater merit than one that appears in a periodical that is regarded as "very ordinary" or "one that publishes almost anything."

In most college departments, writing reviews of books or journal articles will be considered a worthy "add on" to your list of publications, but limiting your writing to book reviews and critiques will fail to earn tenure or promotion.

Summary

Our purpose in the foregoing paragraphs has been to estimate the comparative worth—for purposes of tenure and promotion in rank—of various kinds of publications. It should be apparent that the five kinds we chose in order to illustrate such worth are only a few of the types in academia. Other kinds include ethnographies, autobiographies, memoirs, works of fiction (novels, short stories), journals, reports of experiments and surveys, and more.

THE QUALITY AND QUANTITY OF PUBLICATIONS

A further question of interest to would-be professors is: How much publishing will be expected of me? The answer depends on such conditions as (a) the nature of the higher education institution that employs you, (b) your academic title, (d) the quality of your publications, and (d) the publication records of your colleagues and your competitors.

The Nature of Your College

There is far more pressure to publish frequently in prestigious research universities than in institutions that place their greatest emphasis on teaching, such as private liberal arts colleges and junior colleges. As explained in chapter 2, the passing decades have witnessed a continuing trend for institutions to morph from simpler kinds into ever more complex types. A two-year normal school becomes a four-year teachers college that changes into a liberal arts college that then becomes a university. Or an A&M (agriculture and mechanical arts college) that offers four-year bachelor degrees is changed into a research university with multiple academic disciplines that award master degrees and doctorates. This evolutionary process is accompanied by increased demands for professors to publish. As a consequence, faculty members who wrote little or nothing in the past can find themselves facing publishing expectations that they are not prepared to fulfill. For such people, the rules have changed in the middle of the game.

Your Academic Title

More publishing is expected of tenure-track professors than of faculty members bearing such titles as instructor, lecturer, or adjunct professor, who may profit from salary increases for contributing scholarly writing but are not required to do so.

The Quality of Publications

There is an interaction between the quantity and quality of publications. One publication that makes a great impact on the world's knowledge counts far more toward academic rank than dozens of writings of modest import. For instance, Francis Crick and James Watson would not have had to pen anything more than their discovery of the structure of DNA in order to guarantee them a top rank in a prestigious university. A few publications of modest import will outweigh dozens that are judged to be mere fluff or no more than rewrites of what others have published in the past.

Colleagues and Competitors

Decisions about who receives tenure, promotion in rank, and salary increases are made by your colleagues and administrators. Tenured members of a department typically vote on who deserves tenure or promotion. The department head reports that vote—along with his or her own recommendation—to a dean and perhaps to a campus-wide committee of professors who review the case and send their decision to the president of the institution, who makes the final decision.

Thus, the judgments of a faculty member's peers (colleagues in one's own department and on campus-wide committees) about the quantity and quality of the member's publishing record affect his or her chances for promotion. And those judgments are influenced by those peers' own records. So if you are in a university whose tenured faculty is highly productive—in both quality and quantity of publications—you will face more stringent standards than if your colleagues are less productive.

Furthermore, you will be judged against the records of your competitors. The term competitors here means people to whom you are compared when your are either seeking a teaching job or are already a faculty member who competes with colleagues for rank and salary increases. Your chances of succeeding are affected by the records of those to whom you are being compared.

Continuing Productivity

It is not uncommon for some faculty members to believe that once they have earned tenure, they have sufficiently proven their worth as scholars and thus need publish no more, or at least they need publish only rarely. In effect, they expect regular future advances in rank and salary. However, academia is a hungry beast, requiring constant feeding in the form of more publications and of increasingly impressive ones. To prosper in this atmosphere, you are expected to make research and creative activity a career-long passion.

GETTING YOUR WRITING PUBLISHED

A three-step process in publishing your work consists of (a) finding a suitable publisher or journal, (b) submitting your manuscript, and (c) adjusting to editors' requirements. Because books and journal articles are the principal outlets for academic publishing, the following discussion focuses on those three steps as they apply to books and articles.

Finding a Suitable Book Publisher

It is important to recognize that the specialized academic book industry—other than the textbook field—has fallen on increasingly hard times over the past decade as a result of competition from the Internet and diminishing funds for college libraries. Therefore, it has become more difficult for faculty members to find a willing and traditional print publisher. Many publishing houses are seeking to adjust to these conditions by offering books in both their traditional paper form and as electronic books. Thus, writers of academic books are turning more often to publishing directly on the Internet.

So, how do you find a suitable outlet for your work? The most desirable publisher of your manuscript will be one that issues books in your field of expertise, that is, books well regarded by academicians in your specialty, and particularly a publisher that has a successful marketing record. One way to identify such publishing houses is to browse among books in a college library relating to your topic so as to discover which houses issued them. Then you can consult those publishers' websites on the Internet. The websites will include directions to authors, telling where and how to submit manuscripts.

Another approach consists of using the Internet to search all sorts of university libraries. The search involves (a) entering a library's title into a search engine (such as entering University of Michigan Libraries), (b) then using the general topic or field of your manuscript as a descriptor (such as neutron stars, industrial revolution, John Keats, tea party, or Mayan pottery), and noting the names of publishers that issued the books that seem relevant to your topic.

Finding a Suitable Journal

The same two general methods suggested for finding book publishers are useful in locating journals.

If you browse among journals relating to your academic specialty online or in a college or university library, you can see the sorts of articles that different journals print (topics, length of articles, writing styles). In addition, journals often include—usually inside the back cover—guidelines to authors for sending manuscripts for the editors' consideration.

Submitting a Book Manuscript

If you were writing a novel or a nonfiction book for the general reading audience, you might need to hire a literary agent in order to get a publisher even to look at your work. However, if you are writing a scholarly book aimed primarily at academics and college students, you can approach a publisher on your own.

Then the question becomes: When in the process of writing a book should I contact a publisher? The answer depends on who you are and the topic of your intended tome. Publishers can offer writers a contract at any stage of the creation of a manuscript, ranging from "I've got a great idea" to "Here's the completed manuscript." For example, you could receive a contract on the basis of only a paragraph describing "a great idea" if you already have a distinguished record of publication in your area of expertise and if your subject matter is a "hot topic"—one representing a controversial issue or matter of great import.

But for most authors, more evidence than "a great idea" is needed before a publisher will offer a contract. Editors typically will want (a) a summary of the purpose and general content of the work, (b) a list of chapters, including a précis of each chapter's content, (c) two or three completed chapters that illustrate the writing style, (d) a description of the audience for which the book is intended, and (e) a list of your past publications. The advantage of seeking a contract at this partially completed stage of your book is that the editor can then offer suggestions about ways the final version could be fashioned to improve the quality of the product.

Or, you may choose to complete the entire manuscript before you hunt for a publisher, thereby giving editors a full understanding of what the finished book is intended to be. Furthermore, sending a completed work ensures editors that you can, indeed, finish the job and on time. Book publishers have signed hosts of contracts with professors who have failed to carry through with their commitments or, at best, have delayed sending a completed manuscript until long after the agreed upon deadline.

Submitting an Article to a Journal

Each journal has a particular style in which manuscripts are to be cast. It is necessary to send your manuscript in that form even to have editors to consider it. The way to learn the required style is either by finding the journal's website or else by finding the page at the end of an issue of the journal that describes the required format.

Complying With Book Publishers' Requirements

Conditions that you are expected to fulfill usually appear in three forms—those stipulated in the contract, those in the publisher's style sheet, and others specified by the editors with whom you work.

The principal contents of the contract identify the publisher's rights and responsibilities and the author's rights and responsibilities. Much of the contract focuses on the publisher's rights, which include determining the final form of the book, setting the deadline for a completed manuscript, controlling extended uses of the material (foreign publishers, paperback versions), and protecting the publisher against lawsuits, such as for copyright infringement. The author's rights are usually far fewer, limited to the amount of royalties and perhaps a few free copies of the work upon its publication. In our experience, the size of royalties and number of free copies (perhaps three to six) have diminished over recent decades. And whereas it was not unusual for authors to get 12 percent or 15 percent of the retail price of a book on the first 1,000 copies some decades ago, today the author's share is more likely to be 5 percent to 10 percent. Authors of textbooks that are apt to sell thousands of copies will usually receive a higher royalty rate. Recently we signed a contract for a book on a topic with limited sales potential—social exchange theory. The contract stipulated that no royalties would be paid on the first 500 copies sold, 5 percent 501-to-1000 copies, and gradual increases until at more than 5,000 copies sold the royalty would reach 9 percent.

It's apparent that writing academic books is rarely a highly financially profitable venture. Any financial benefit you derive from publishing will not come in the form of royalties. It will be in the form of salary increases you receive as a result of promotion in rank that is based on your success publishing books and journal articles.

Complying With Journal Editors' Requirements

Editors' main requirements appear in the style sheet for the journal, but there can be other expectations as well. Journal editors typically have four choices in their treatment of your manuscript. They can (a) publish your submission with no changes, (b) require minor changes before accepting it, (c) require major changes before accepting it, or (d) reject it outright. In the case of refereed journals, the editor sends a copy of your manuscript to two or three experts in the academic field of your article, asking them to assess your work's strengths and weaknesses. Then the editor informs you of the referees' opinions and states that, before the piece will be published, you need to remedy any faults the referees found in your manuscript

Summary

As explained earlier, publishing respected scholarship is not only considered desirable in higher education institutions, but it is a necessity in an increasing number of colleges and universities. The purpose of this first section of the chapter has been to inform prospective professors of (a) the types of publications most valued by administrators and faculty members who make decisions about tenure, promotion, and salary; and (b) where and how to get one's writings published.

PERFORMING

Performances consist of faculty members appearing before an audience to display their skills. The display may be either live or recorded. In a live performance, the audience witnesses the action as it occurs. In its recorded form, the event is heard or seen as an audiotape, videotape, compact disc, radio broadcast, television broadcast, Internet transmission, or the like.

Performances can assume many forms—speeches, debates, demonstrations, literary readings, musical presentations, dramas, dances, and athletic contests. In the following section, rather than attempting to analyze every type in the entire range of performances, we inspect in detail a single case, then extract from that case a series of generalizations applicable to all kind of performances.

The illustrative case concerns a tenured faculty member in his fifties, Dr. Leonard L. Garrison, in the Lionel Hampton School of Music at the University of Idaho. The analysis offers answers to three questions that we believe are of particular interest to graduate students who contemplate a career as a tenure-track professor: (a) What has been the nature of the professor's performances? (b) How did the professor acquire the opportunities to perform? (c) How did different performances compare in the value or worth assigned to them by the people who typically make decisions about a faculty member's tenure, academic rank, and salary?

At the outset, we should explain a bit about Dr. Garrison's situation. He entered his present position by a less common route than that taken by most professors of music. The typical route consists of an individual seeking a full-time academic career immediately after completing graduate school. However, during most of the three decades before Dr. Garrison joined the University of Idaho faculty, his principal occupation had been that of a symphony orchestra flute and piccolo musician, plus part-time teaching in nearby universities. He had performed for fourteen years with the Tulsa (Oklahoma) Philharmonic until the orchestra was disbanded, a victim of the depressed economy. Over those years, Dr.

Garrison's wife, Dr. Shannon Scott, had served as the Philharmonic's principal clarinetist. The pair then decided to become full-time faculty members, he at the University of Idaho and she at nearby Washington State University. The pair has often performed together as the Scott/Garrison Duo.

The following account focuses on Dr. Garrison's record of performances during his first five years in Idaho, 2006–2010.

The Nature of Performances

Earlier, we identified three types of activity that might be considered by an administrator or committee that was assessing applicants for a faculty appointment, for tenure, or for promotion in rank or salary. The three were teaching, service, and creative activity. By far the most important of the three is creative activity, which, in Dr. Garrison's case, was that of playing the flute or piccolo before an audience or at a recording session. That is the type on which the following analysis focuses. Two other activities—which some committees might regard more as service to the profession than as creative activity—are those of appraising other musicians' performances (writing critical reviews, judging contests) and of organizing events (recitals, music conventions, summer music camps).

When candidates for a college teaching job or for promotion in rank present their record of performances, they are wise to organize the material in a form that is (a) easily comprehended and (b) identifies kinds of performance that are usually assigned different values by people who review the record. The following list uses the scheme in which Dr. Garrison cast his record at the close of his first five years on the University of Idaho faculty. For each type over the five-year span, we show the number of performances (in parentheses) along with one example to suggest the variety of venues in which he performed. The categories are recordings, radio broadcasts, concerto soloist, recitals, and orchestral performances.

- Recordings. Each of Dr. Garrison's four compact discs consisted of a series of musical selections. Three were for flute and piccolo with piano accompaniment (*Superflute, American Reflections, East Meets West*). The fourth (*Barn Dance*) featured clarinet/flute duets with Dr. Shannon Scott on the clarinet.
- Radio Broadcasts. National Public Radio (4) and regional (12), as on Wisconsin Public Radio and on Yellowstone Public Radio.

- Concerto Soloist with Orchestras. National (2), as with the Blue Lake Festival Band, and regional/local (4) as with the Walla Walla Symphony.
- Recitals, Invited—Solo and Chamber Music. National (14), such as the College Music Society National Conference; regional (21), as in a Seattle Flute Society concert.
- Recitals, Local—Solo and Chamber Music (39), as University of Idaho Faculty Chamber Music.
- Orchestral Performances. National (5), as in the Blue Lake Festival Orchestra; regional (11), as at an Idaho-Washington Chorale concert.

Opportunities to Perform

Musicians can either be invited to perform or they can apply to perform. If there are multiple candidates applying, they usually will need to audition, that is, to display their musicianship in the form of a recording or a live performance. The individuals who are judged most skilled during the auditions are the ones accepted for the event.

If there are many more applicants than can be accommodated, then the sponsors of the event may need to limit the number of individuals that audition. Many opportunities in the arts are screened through an anonymous process. For example, a musician may be chosen from a blind listening of numerous performances. The event sponsors, in making their decision, may also turn to information about the applicants' backgrounds. That information can include the applicants' music education, such as which music schools they attended and their academic degrees. In Dr. Garrison's case, he graduated from the Oberlin Conservatory of Music (BM), State University of New York at Stony Brook (MM), and Northwestern University (DM). His wife, Dr. Shannon Scott, attended Julliard (BM), École Normale de Musique de Paris, Conservatoire Regional Marcel Dupré, Yale University (MM), and Northwestern University (DM). In addition, event sponsors may seek information about applicants' previous performances and scholarships or awards they received.

There are various ways professors discover opportunities to perform. One way is to become a member of organizations in one's specialization. For example, Dr. Garrison has been a member of nine professional music organizations, ranging from the National Flute Association (6,000 members), through the College Music Society and the Music Educators National Conference, to the Seattle Flute Society. His memberships not only informed him of chances to appear at those groups' events but also helped him establish friendships with colleagues who could offer opportunities.

As a husband-and-wife team, Drs. Garrison and Scott enhanced their opportunities by including each other in performance events at their respective schools.

The roles that musicians assume in professional societies can also affect their performance chances. For instance, in the National Flute Association over the past decade, Dr. Garrison advanced from secretary to treasurer and in 2008–2010 to the top post of chair of the board of directors. As a result, he became known to an ever-widening range of flutists and event sponsors.

Additional chances to perform are found in publications of musical occasions, including announcements appearing on the Internet where venues for flutists can be found by entering such descriptors as flute events, flute competitions, and flute opportunities into a search engine.

The Comparative Value of Different Performances

As explained earlier in this chapter, not all publications by faculty members are judged of equal scholarly value; some are considered more prestigious than others. The same is true of performances. To illustrate this point, we analyze Dr. Garrison's record of recordings and of live appearances before an audience.

Recordings

A collection of a dozen or more musical selections on a compact disc is particularly valued by members of search or promotion committees. Not only can the members listen to the musician's work, but they will be impressed by the fact that a record company has judged the work of sufficient quality to be purchased by a discriminating public. There are two main ways to produce recordings. Either a musician can pay to have the records made or a recording company can issue the work. Even if such a company has agreed to issue the recording, the musician must bear costs of production. If the performer has received grant support, some—or, in rare cases, all—of the costs are covered. Usually the performer supports the project in part or in full with personal funds. The second of these options—a respected label—is by far the preferred method, especially if the recording company has a reputation for music of high quality. The four compact discs of Dr. Garrison's recordings were produced under well-regarded labels—Albany Records, Centaur Records, and Capstone Records.

Not only is it desirable to have recordings issued by a publisher rather than being self-produced, it is also helpful to have music critics' opinions of the work available to members of search or promotion committees. For instance, a critic's review in *Fanfare Magazine* of the Scott/Garrison Duo's *Barn Dance* disc included such comments as:

> Shannon Scott and Leonard Garrison have put together an enticing recital of gems, all world premiere recordings, and every one of them a winner. . . . In the hands of these two wonderful artists, more colors are evoked than one might believe possible. . . . The consummate artistry and polished ensemble-playing of the Scott/Garrison Duo as heard on this disc ought to win them many admirers. (Canfield, 2011, pp. 159–60)

A reviewer of *American Reflections* in the periodical *The Flute Network* wrote:

> Garrison's playing combines great virtuosity, superb control of musical expression, and high energy with lyricism. He makes the most difficult technical passage seem easy, and extreme dynamics and wide leaps appear effortless. It is quickly evident on the Beaser Souvenirs that he is a specialist on the piccolo, and the other works show him throughout at his flutistic best with a clear, focused, and singing tone throughout the range of the instrument. (Pritchard, 2009, para. 2)

Live Performances

From our analysis of Dr. Garrison's appearances before audiences, we propose five principles that appear to influence the esteem in which different sorts of concerts are held by college administrators, search committees, and promotion committees:

- The more extensive the audience, the more prestigious the performance. Hence, an international audience is better than a national one, a national audience is better than a regional one, and a regional audience is better than a local one.

- Appearing as a soloist is more highly valued than appearing as a member of a duet or small chamber music group, and being in a chamber group counts more than being in a large orchestra.
- The more innovative the performance, the greater credit given to the musician for originality. (For instance, the *Barn Dance* disc represented the first recording of each selection on the disc.)
- Being invited to perform is more desirable than having to apply and audition for the opportunity.
- Reports of music critics' favorable opinions of a musician's work impress committee members.

The following examples from Dr. Garrison's record illustrate how those principles may interact to determine the value that committee members assign to four events that descend in value from the most prestigious (Japan tour), to the second most significant (solo recital tour), through a third (Walla Walla Symphony), and finally to the least significant (faculty chamber music concerts on campus).

Tour of Japan. Before joining the University of Idaho faculty, Dr. Garrison in 2003 was a musician with the Chicago Symphony Orchestra that played a series of concerts in Japan. Prior to that time, he was in the flute section of the Chicago Civic Orchestra, which was the training orchestra for the symphony. He had earned the place in the Civic Orchestra through competitive audition and, when the symphony needed an additional flute, he was often added to the roster. In terms of prestige, the Japan tour would rate high for (a) representing multiple concert appearances in an international setting, (b) the symphony's international stature as one of the top orchestras, and (c) Dr. Garrison's having been invited to join the tour. He would have been given even greater credit if he had been a featured soloist rather than being just another member of the orchestra.

Solo Recital Tour. In 2011, Dr. Garrison performed as a soloist at five universities in three states (Florida, Louisiana, Mississippi), a tour that included a national conference at the University of Florida. This set of events would be expected to rank high in the judgments of promotion committee members because he had been invited as a soloist at a national level to perform a program of varied and challenging musical selections.

Walla Walla (Washington) Symphony. In a series of four concerts during 2010–2011, Dr. Garrison served as the orchestra's principal flutist, a position normally earned through auditioning, in this case by invitation from the orchestra's music director. Those performances would certainly count to his credit but would not be valued as highly as the Japan and solo recital tours because (a) the Walla Walla Symphony was regional and not of the stature of the Chicago Symphony and (b) Dr. Garrison had been the featured soloist in the recitals at sites in three states.

Faculty Chamber Music. We have judged this event to be the least prestigious of our four examples because the performance—featuring faculty members within the University of Idaho's school of music—was local, limited to the university campus.

PRODUCTS

As noted earlier, products are observable items (other than print publications) that faculty members create. The types of products indicative of a faculty member's creativity vary from one academic field to another. In a geology department, the product might be a computer program designed to simulate the earth's climatic conditions fifty years from now. In a physics department the item could be an improved spectrometer for carbon-dating objects collected during space flights. For a school of music, it might be a composition, such as a violin concerto or symphony. In a physical education department it could be an improved football helmet that would reduce head injuries. In a civil engineering school, the invention could be fireproof shingles constructed from worn-out auto tires. In a home economics department it could be novel dress designs. In an art department, evidence of creativity could be in the form of various kinds of objects, such as drawings, paintings, photographs, motion pictures, carvings, ceramics, sculptures, and fabrics.

For faculty members in tenure-track positions, the value of their products is typically judged by how well their creative effort meets such criteria as originality, quality, impact, and productivity.

Originality means how different the object is from other objects of the same type; the more ways in which the object is different from others, the better. However, an item's just being different is of no significance at all if the item is considered to be of low quality.

Quality is what a particular individual (the person who is doing the judging, such as a fellow faculty member) values in the type of object at hand. Thus, what constitutes quality can differ significantly from one judge to the next. In assessing a musical composition, a professor of music who holds classical styles (Bach, Beethoven, Brahms) in high regard might dismiss a series of rap compositions as being of poor quality, whereas another professor might laud the rap creations as highly valued reflections of modern life experiences. A promotions committee member who highly values lifelike realism in sculpture will assign a low quality score to a stick with a ball on top that is labeled "Tall Man." Yet another member of the committee who valorizes uncommon analogies between the human form and unlikely objects may deem the stick-and-ball creation a brilliant innovation.

Impact is judged by the range of influence the product has exerted or will likely exert. The more people that the product will influence, the greater the innovation's worth.

Productivity concerns how many objects the faculty member creates. Is an item the only one the faculty member has produced, or is it only one of a series devised over time?

In summary, the faculty members who can expect the fastest promotion on the tenure ladder are ones whose products are the most original, are highest in quality, exert the broadest impact, and appear frequently.

To illustrate how a tenure-track faculty member's products may be judged for the purpose of appointment or promotion, we will use the following hypothetical case. Imagine that we are members of a search committee assigned to assess three potential candidates for a top-notch professorship in the art department of our university. The purpose of the appointment is to add instant splendor to the art department by appointing a distinguished specialist in drawing and painting. Thus, we need to judge the comparative worth of hypothetical applicants' products—their drawings and paintings. We then try to rank these potential candidates in terms of how valuable they likely would be for bringing glory to our art faculty. But we also need to identify what additional information we would want about their products in order to refine how they should be ranked.

Here are brief summaries of descriptions of three fictitious candidates. Following the summaries, we offer our judgments of those professors' products in terms originality, quality, impact, and productivity.

Candidate A: Earned a bachelor-of-fine-arts degree (BFA) from a lesser-known mid-western art college and her master-of-fine-arts degree (MFA) from a well-known East Coast university. She has had five solo exhibits in the United States at galleries of moderate reputation and has had her work shown in other exhibitions at two lesser-known galleries in the mid-west and three well-known West Coast galleries. Her work is part of the permanent collections of five public East Coast galleries.

Candidate B: Earned a BFA from a West Coast University of moderate reputation and a MFA from a well-known West Coast university. She has numerous solo international exhibitions, including shows at several major US galleries and galleries in France, Italy, Spain, and the Netherlands. Her work has been described in major newspapers and several art magazines. Her paintings are in permanent collections in several major US galleries. She has served as visiting professor at one major university in the United States and several in Europe.

Candidate C: Received her BFA and MFA degrees from a major university. She has had sixteen solo exhibitions throughout the West Coast at local galleries of modest reputation.

A Decision Making Process

With these descriptions in hand, we are now prepared to arrive at a tentative decision about how to rank the three professors according to our four standards—originality, quality, impact, and productivity.

Originality. We are unable to judge originality directly. To do so, we would need to (a) see each artist's drawings and paintings and (b) have in mind the drawings and paintings of a wide variety of other artists, past and present, so as to estimate how innovative our candidates' works are in comparison to earlier artists' products. However, as an alternative approach, we can estimate the candidates' originality if we are willing to assume that respected art museums and art dealers will neither exhibit nor purchase paintings that are essentially copies of existing paintings' subject matter, styles, and media. On the basis of such an assumption, we can rank our candidates according to the number of exhibits and purchases of their work in well-regarded museums and art shows.

Quality. What constitutes quality in art is a highly controversial matter. Art historians, art critics, art dealers, art gallery personnel, art museum personnel, and artists themselves often disagree about what constitutes quality. Furthermore, their opinions are frequently at odds with views expressed by members of the general public. Therefore, whose opinions do we accept for judging our three candidates? Because the purpose of this appointment is to add glory to our university's art department, we would be prudent to accept the judgments of art critics and museum personnel. That judgment is reflected in the sorts of paintings exhibited and purchased by prestigious museums, galleries, and art dealers.

Impact. As noted earlier, impact is judged by the range of influence the product has exerted or will likely exert. The more people that the paintings influence in a wide range of venues, the greater the product's impact. And for our purpose of bringing glory to our university's art department, we particularly value impressing people who are considered to be "art experts."

Productivity. The candidate we recommend for appointment should not be one who is satisfied to rest on her laurels, that is, to feel that the paintings she has produced and exhibited in the past warrant her receiving tenure and earn future promotions. Instead, we want one who is continually creating new works. Evidence of productivity can be in the form of the quantity of exhibits and purchases of the artist's products.

A Tentative Ranking

On the basis of our decision-making process we rank Candidate B at the top, well ahead of the other two professors. We put Candidate A in second place and Candidate C in third place on the basis of the following line of reasoning.

Candidate B, compared to A and C, has (a) had more paintings in the permanent collections of prestigious museums, (b) exhibits in a greater variety of venues world-wide, (c) has had more articles about her work in more publications. She has been a visiting professor at major universities.

Candidate A, whom we ranked in second place, had (a) fewer paintings exhibited in less renowned sites and only within the United States, and (b) had paintings in the permanent collections of less distinguished venues. There is no evidence that her work has been written about in newspapers or in art publications, or that she has been invited to serve as a visiting scholar in noteworthy universities.

Candidate C, whom we relegated to third place, had a record of numerous solo exhibits, but nearly all of them were at minor galleries. There is no evidence that her work has been written about in newspapers or in art publications, or that she has been invited to serve as a visiting scholar in other universities.

To refine our tentative rankings of the three hypothetical professors' creative work, we can seek additional evidence by asking each of the candidates to send us a complete curriculum vitae, which we expect would include more pertinent information about their creative work than the lists of products that we rank here.

FINDING TIME FOR RESEARCH AND CREATIVE ACTIVITY

A problem faculty members in research universities often face is that of having sufficient time to fulfill their creative activity responsibilities when they are carrying substantial teaching, service, and student-advising burdens. One way to find extra time is to use the summer vacation for intensive work on your research agenda. Another is to obtain financial grants that allow you to "buy time" during the academic year—that is, to obtain funds that can be used by your department to pay for an instructor who can take over part or all of your teaching load. A third way is to apply for a sabbatical leave.

The word sabbatical can be traced back several millennia to its use in the Judaic Torah (the Old Testament of the Christian Bible) where sabbatical meant "ceasing" as in God's ceasing to work on the seventh day of the creation of the universe. Hence, Sabbath became a day of relief from ordinary labor. In present day higher education institutions, a sabbatical leave is an opportunity for faculty members to be relieved of their usual duties in order to further develop their expertise and renew themselves professionally. A professor's being awarded a sabbatical leave is perhaps the most highly valued way to find time for research and other creative endeavors.

Policies governing sabbatical leaves vary somewhat from one nation to another and from one institution to another. However, there are several policies that are quite widespread. For instance, sabbaticals are usually available only to full-time professors, often granted only to tenured faculty members after they have compiled a certain number of years of service. In the United States, that number is typically at least six years of full-time teaching, with the recipient freed of usual duties throughout the seventh year. In many institutions, a faculty member can take either a half-year's leave at full salary or a full year's at half salary. Sabbaticals are rarely guaranteed, but granted only if the faculty member is deemed to have earned the privilege through high quality work and if the department can arrange to carry out the professor's teaching and service responsibilities. The typical nature of requirements can be illustrated with the policy in New York University's Steinhardt School of Culture, Education, and Human Development:

> Sabbatical leave for the purpose of pursuing professional activities designed to enhance subsequent service to the University may be granted to full-time members of the faculty who have attained tenure and completed a minimum of six years of full-time service to the University. It is granted as a privilege, rather than right, which should result in minimal disruption of institutional programs and no additional cost to the School or University. It is not granted automatically on the basis of years of service and tenure status. A sabbatical leave provides the faculty member with opportunity to undertake desirable professional activities with which the pressures of a regular "load" would interfere. Sabbatical activities should represent an extension of the faculty member's career to date or an effort at career reorientation. Such leaves generally involve scholarly research, study, or other creative endeavors relevant to the specialty of the faculty member and the goals of the institution. All sabbatical leave arrangements approved by the University carry the restriction that the faculty member is not permitted to engage in any form of regular academic or other employment to augment income during the sabbatical. (Sabbatical leave, 2014)

During their sabbatical periods, professors may pursue various activities—collect research data, write journal articles, write a book, prepare a new course, collaborate with colleagues at other institutions, give performances in various sites (musical, dramatic, dance), or pursue advanced study at a different university. They often serve as visiting professors or guest researchers at institutions other than their own. You might arrange to teach a course or give a series of guest lectures in exchange for the use of an office while you are a visitor at another university. Some institutions have funds for paying you as a visiting professor or guest researcher.

One way to arrange for a visiting professorship or the chance to conduct cooperative research away from your own institution is through your professional contacts, such as colleagues from other campuses whom you meet at professional societies' conferences. Another source of opportunities is the Internet where you find information by entering such descriptors as fellowships, sabbaticals, and visiting professorships into a search engine. For example, consider this excerpt from the Fulbright website:

The Fulbright Program, the U.S. Government's flagship international educational exchange program, is designed to increase mutual understanding between the people of the United States and the people of other countries. The Fulbright Program provides participants—chosen for their academic merit and leadership potential—with the opportunity to study, teach and conduct research, exchange ideas, and contribute to finding solutions to shared international concerns. . . . The Fulbright Program operates in more than 155 countries worldwide and has provided approximately 325,000 participants with the opportunity to study, teach or conduct research in each others' countries and exchange ideas. (Fulbright, 2012, para, 1, 3)

If you intend to apply for a sabbatical leave, it is wise to begin planning months or even over a year ahead of time (such as when applying for a Fulbright), since you typically will be required to submit a detailed description of how you aim to spend your leave time. Not only does your department chairperson have to make arrangements for covering your teaching and service responsibilities in your absence, but you need to convince administrators that your sabbatical activities will indeed be academically productive. When you complete your sabbatical, you'll generally have to submit a sabbatical completion memo, describing what you have done, and you will owe your university a certain period of time (e.g., a year) before you can change jobs or move to another university.

CONCLUSION

The contents of this chapter are most important for individuals interested in a tenure-track teaching career in universities that include research and creative activity as an essential element of their missions. However, in recent decades as more four-year colleges and two-year community colleges have assigned increasing value to publishing, performing, and products, the topics featured in this chapter have become increasingly significant for faculty members whose progress in the profession formerly depended solely on the quality of their teaching and service responsibilities.

SEVEN
Teaching

At most colleges and universities, your teaching role will be central to your faculty duties. In some colleges, your teaching will actually be your primary or major duty, as in many community colleges and private universities. Thus, you will be expected to teach more classes and may have little or no research or creative activity expectation. In other higher education institutions (such as Research I universities), research and creative or scholarly activity is central and teaching might be of equivalent status or more of a secondary duty. Thus, professors in such institutions might teach fewer courses (or sometimes no courses at all) but be held to higher expectations for research productivity, grants, etc. Such institutions are likely to highly value renowned researchers that they can count among their ranks. However, most higher education institutions value some combination of teaching and research.

Even if teaching is only a secondary duty, it is to your benefit (marketability) to develop effective teaching skills, which can serve you well in a variety of contexts, such as presenting your research at conferences.

In this chapter, we provide several suggestions to consider as you begin teaching. In a separate volume, *A Guide to College and University Teaching* (Iding and Thomas, in press) we address issues related to teaching in depth. Here are several suggestions.

- As you interview for positions, ask about teaching loads and expectations. You need to determine for yourself the optimal balance of teaching and research.

- When you accept a position (or before, while interviewing), inquire about course reductions for new faculty or other benefits, such as teaching a course that you've already taught or one that's directly in your area of expertise. Teaching more than one section of the same course can also reduce your course preparation time.

- In preparing to teach for the first time, ask the department chair or colleagues in your area for sample syllabi. Find out if there are requirements that need to be covered in the course, and what choices you have in terms of compiling readings, ordering books, getting materials copied for students.

- Find out as much as you can about your students beforehand so you can aim your instruction appropriately.

- Join faculty development seminars or new faculty mentoring programs that facilitate teaching improvement. Many universities have units expressly for faculty teaching development, such as a Center for Teaching Excellence. Examine their online offerings and handbooks for new instructors and sign up for workshops and teaching seminars.

- Be videotaped while teaching. While many of us dread to see ourselves on video, we can learn a great deal about how to improve our teaching. And the video can help us to contextualize students' comments on teaching evaluations.

- Learn about different teaching strategies and instructional innovations—and the related research that supports them—related to teaching your subject matter. For example, have students in large lectures take a few minutes to discuss a concept with others sitting near them. Try clickers (audience response or student response systems). In other classes, try using small groups to solve problems. Try out problem-based learning. Use games to review for tests or peer responses to improve writing. There are infinite ways to add to your instructional repertoire, and reading books about teaching in higher education, and journals about teaching in your discipline can provide a wealth of ideas.

- Most colleges will require some sort of course evaluation. Perhaps there is one used throughout your department or college. Save your evaluations and note trends of improvement. To complement the evaluations, you might invite other faculty members (preferably senior to you), to sit in on your classes and write memos summarizing the experience. All of these can be used to help document your teaching improvement when you apply for promotion and tenure.

- Consider teaching a process of growth. You might not be expected to be "perfect" on day one, but treat each subsequent day as a learning experience. Determine what your strengths are as instructor (e.g., leading group discussions, lecturing) and capitalize on those. Determine your areas for improvement and work on them.

CONCLUSION

As described in this chapter, most faculty members' responsibilities include teaching. We provided some brief suggestions that should help you to (a) consider the degree to which teaching should be part of your ideal faculty position, (b) get started as a new instructor, and (c) recognize that learning to teach well is a process of continual development and growth.

EIGHT

Service Obligations

While instruction and creative activity (especially research) are at the heart of most university faculty positions, you may be surprised by the numerous service obligations that go with your position, such as faculty committees, student advising, requests to speak at community events, and membership in professional societies. So the question arises: How do you effectively navigate among your obligations without over-committing yourself to service tasks? In this chapter we discuss this third major category of faculty responsibility—service—that follows teaching and research.

FACULTY COMMITTEE SERVICE

At the outset of your appointment to the faculty, you are likely to be invited to serve on at least one or two committees—curriculum, admissions, scholarship, or others. How do you determine which committees are effective commitments of your time and expertise? How do you decline committee service when it interferes with other teaching and research obligations?

Generally, departments have a number of service obligations that they need to fulfill to run smoothly. Decisions need to be made about which students to admit, whom to hire, curricular changes in courses, and course scheduling and teaching assignments. If you are in a small department, your department chair might do a number of these functions, or you may be involved in all of them to some extent along with the whole department. In larger departments, separate committees may be assigned to deal with each of these functions.

Beyond departmental obligations, you may be recruited to serve on college-wide committees by your dean or the dean's equivalent. Perhaps admissions are handled at the college level for all of the departments, or there might be a scholarship committee that evaluates student scholarship applications. Further, you might have a college-wide faculty senate with officers, representatives, and separate committees involved with different aspects of faculty governance, such as personnel, curriculum, and diversity committees.

And there are other areas of faculty service. There are university-wide committees as well. For example, at the University of Hawai'i at Mānoa a university-wide faculty senate has committees for assessment, student affairs, academic policy/planning, academic grievances, and athletics among others. There are other committees related to planning, tenure, promotion, enrollment, and college accreditation.

Community Service

In addition to departmental, college, and university service, you can engage in service to your community and to your profession. Community service generally relates to the city or region in which your institution is situated. If you are an expert on Japanese woodblock prints during the Edo period, you could be invited to lecture at a local art exhibit. If you are a scientist, you could be asked to help judge high school science projects, or serve on a committee or board of directors related to your local science museum or aquarium. As a special education expert, you might provide a lecture to parents on your research on autism.

Service to Your Profession

You will be expected to engage in service to your profession. This involves being active in organizations related to your academic specialization, such as the American Psychological Association, the Mathematical Association of America, or the Institute of Electrical and Electronics Engineers. Here, you go beyond merely presenting your research at well-respected, refereed conferences. You can take an active role in the association's operations. It's useful to become active by joining special interest groups within larger organizations, serving as a reviewer of conference proposals, becoming a committee member, or serving as an officer for your special interest group. Further, you may serve as a reviewer of journal articles in your research area or as a member of an editorial board. These kinds of roles are especially helpful in furthering your career when you apply for promotion and tenure, as you will need to solicit reviewers of your work and demonstrate leadership within your profession. Thus, through such activities you make yourself and your work known within your professional community and create connections with peers interested in similar research, peers who are likely to be closely tied to your specific area of expertise than your colleagues at your institution.

MANAGING MULTIPLE ROLES

So, how do you navigate all of these potential obligations, especially when you might be quite busy developing a research agenda and teaching new courses? Following are some suggestions that may help you manage your service obligations.

Engage in service opportunities that capitalize on your expertise. If your research area or other expertise truly enables you to make a unique contribution in your community, perhaps by giving a talk or serving on a board, you might find the experience quite rewarding. Also, universities and departments usually value the publicity that can be associated with faculty members' work and expertise.

Select opportunities that will facilitate your professional growth and reputation. For example, participating as an officer in your special interest group or serving on the editorial board of a journal are good ways to do so. At the present time, when many new online journals are springing up, it is wise to be selective by choosing to work with journals and organizations that are well respected.

If you have administrative ambitions (you want to eventually be a department chair, dean, or other administrator) you might solicit opportunities in which you can interact regularly with administrators at your institution or with officers in your profession. Thus, you can gain experience in administrative roles.

Weigh the amount of time, professional benefit to your career, and departmental or other political loyalties you need to maintain when agreeing to service roles. For example, you might be asked to serve on a student admissions or scholarship committee and find yourself reading and rating dozens of applications and spending numerous hours in related meetings—and if you do a good job, you are likely to be asked to serve on the committee again! We have served on these kinds of committees and found them quite rewarding, so we are not decrying service activities. Often departmental service obligations are rotated within the faculty, so members take turns serving on committees. But you need to weigh the amount of time you are likely to put into service compared to the time you need for teaching and research and creative activity, since those are the more important responsibilities for furthering your career.

Don't neglect service related to your teaching. As an instructor or professor, you will be expected to carry out teaching related service obligations. These include holding regular office hours, advising students, and overseeing students' theses or dissertation research. In some institutions, you bear that overseer responsibility only after you have served on the faculty for a while or have compiled a significant record of publication or other creative work.

It is also important to learn how many office hours you're required to hold for students and to post the schedule clearly on your office door, to list them in the syllabi for your classes, and to make them known to your department secretary or other administrative staff. In addition, inform students of how best to reach you by phone or email. And if you're not able to meet students at a regularly posted time, let them know when alternate office hours will be held.

When you feel that you must turn down a service request, do so in a polite and diplomatic way. For instance, if you find that you are being asked to participate in service to the extent that it interferes with your teaching or research obligations, or if you are being asked to undertake significantly more service than are other new faculty members, you are wise to explain in a discrete fashion that your present research, teaching, and service activities have already filled the time you have available. It is appropriate to express thanks for the invitation and possible interest in future service. Sometimes faculty members find themselves asked to serve on a number of committees because of a particular expertise they possess or because they fit a particular demographic profile, such as you would be the only female or only statistician or only member of an ethnic group who adds diversity to a committee. In such an event, you are obliged to weigh potential benefits of such a contribution against your other obligations.

Particularly when you are a new faculty member, your colleagues and department chair can help you decide which service responsibilities it is wise to accept in terms of your current workload and long-term career.

Enjoy your service opportunities. You may find that some of your contributions to service (selecting scholarship winners, working with a community organization, joining a professional society) to be among your most rewarding activities. You might reassess the value of your professional expertise and its usefulness in addressing concrete needs. In addition, you can gain valuable insight to how your community, university, and profession really function; and you can establish valued friendships outside of your departmental circle.

CONCLUSION

As described in this chapter, faculty members' responsibilities include activities that (a) contribute to the efficient operation of their higher learning institution, (b) improve the communities they inhabit—local, state, national—and (c) support their profession, particularly the academic field in which they specialize.

III

Influential Issues

We estimate that most individuals who consider becoming a college or university faculty member are not aware of a variety of ethical and legal matters that can affect a professor's fate. Nor are they likely to recognize how power struggles among members of a higher education institution can influence the course of their lives, including their promotion and tenure. The three chapters in part III have been designed to help prepare aspirants to cope with such issues. Chapter 9 focuses on ethical and legal concerns, chapter 10 on professorial politics, and chapter 11 on promotion and tenure.

NINE

Ethical and Legal Concerns

In this chapter we do not provide an exhaustive description of all ethical or legal areas that faculty members can profitably understand. Instead, we limit our description to several issues about which faculty members should be knowledgeable. Such matters are often presumed to be common knowledge—or common sense—among personnel, but they may not be.

When writing this chapter, we consulted several sources: (a) our own experiences, (b) an interview with a union administrator who represents faculty members in difficult situations, and (c) descriptions of ethical principles advocated by such organizations as the American Association of University Professors (AAUP)—the latter organization of which we relied upon heavily in this chapter. Although we describe issues, we do not pretend to offer legal advice about any particular type of case.

AN AAUP STATEMENT

We begin with the American Association of University Professors' Statement on Professorial Ethics (AAUP, 2009) that proposes basic principles bearing on intellectual honesty, respectful treatment of students and colleagues, and avoidance of conflict-of-interest in business, political, or other arenas external to professors' university work.

> Professors, guided by a deep conviction of the worth and dignity of the advancement of knowledge, recognize the special responsibilities placed upon them. Their primary responsibility to their subject is to

seek and to state the truth as they see it. To this end, professors devote their energies to developing and improving their scholarly competence. They accept the obligation to exercise critical self-discipline and judgment in using, extending, and transmitting knowledge. They practice intellectual honesty. Although professors may follow subsidiary interests, these interests must never seriously hamper or compromise their freedom of inquiry.

As teachers, professors encourage the free pursuit of learning in their students. They hold before them the best scholarly and ethical standards of their discipline. Professors demonstrate respect for students as individuals and adhere to their proper roles as intellectual guides and counselors. Professors make every reasonable effort to foster honest academic conduct and to ensure that their evaluations of students reflect each student's true merit. They respect the confidential nature of the relationship between professor and student. They avoid any exploitation, harassment, or discriminatory treatment of students. They acknowledge significant academic or scholarly assistance from them. They protect their academic freedom.

As colleagues, professors have obligations that derive from common membership in the community of scholars. Professors do not discriminate against or harass colleagues. They respect and defend the free inquiry of associates, even when it leads to findings and conclusions that differ from their own. Professors acknowledge academic debt and strive to be objective in their professional judgment of colleagues. Professors accept their share of faculty responsibilities for the governance of their institution.

As members of an academic institution, professors seek above all to be effective teachers and scholars. Although professors observe the stated regulations of the institution, provided the regulations do not contravene academic freedom, they maintain their right to criticize and seek revision. Professors give due regard to their paramount responsibilities within their institution in determining the amount and character of work done outside it. When considering the interruption or termination of their service, professors recognize the effect of their decision upon the program of the institution and give due notice of their intentions.

As members of their community, professors have the rights and obligations of other citizens. Professors measure the urgency of these obligations in the light of their responsibilities to their subject, to their students, to their profession, and to their institution. When they speak or act as private persons, they avoid creating the impression of speaking or acting for their college or university. As citizens engaged in a profession that depends upon freedom for its health and integrity, professors have a particular obligation to promote conditions of free inquiry and to further public understanding of academic freedom. (AAUP, 2009. Reprinted with permission from the American Association of University Professors)

SPECIFIC ETHICAL ISSUES

Beyond general ethical policies, faculty members may be obliged to deal with other issues that can pose ethical dilemmas and about which they should be knowledgeable such as (a) requiring students to use particular learning materials, (b) plagiarism, (d) conflicts of interest, (e) intellectual property, and (f) copyright and fair use.

Assigning One's Own Text Materials

Although you might have written a book or authored other materials in response to a need to provide a better text for your students, the altruism behind that goal can be compromised by what some critics view as financial gain for yourself (AAUP, 2004). Some universities address this issue directly. For example, you may be required to donate any financial remuneration you receive as a result of textbook sales to students in your classes to a scholarship fund or some other fund at your university, or you may have to apply for permission to require your book from a university committee or administrator. The "profit" you actually earn may be quite small indeed. For example, some publishers today do not provide any compensation to academic authors until they have sold a certain number of books.

Plagiarism

The AAUP (1990c) cautions against plagiarism of the sort that most students are made fully aware of before and during secondary schools and in postsecondary institutions. Beyond knowing discipline-specific methods for acknowledging sources, they recommend that professors ensure that their higher education institutions have clearly articulated guidelines for handling plagiarism and penalties. Thus, familiarizing yourself with institutional guidelines and procedures is recommended. Furthermore, the document urges faculty members to model integrity in their own research practices, specifically acknowledging the contributions of students to research. We also suggest articulating conventions for authorship that you adhere to at the initiation of research collaborations with students and other faculty members, to prevent possible disappointments and resentment.

Conflicts of Interest

As university faculty are encouraged to be more entrepreneurial in seeking external funding and in partnering with the corporate world, potential conflicts of interest can arise. Two documents that are valuable in addressing such issues are *Statement of Conflicts of Interest* (AAUP, 2013) and *On Preventing Conflicts of Interest in Government-Sponsored Research at Universities* (AAUP, 1990a). The National Science Foundation (2005), as a sponsor of many funded research projects, also has offered a useful policy statement.

Reading these documents raises questions that faculty members who contemplate embarking on such ventures can usefully consider, including: Would I feel pressured to present research findings in such a way that the interests of the funding source are supported? In other words, will the funding source affect the research outcome? Would I or my academic department that obtains such funding enjoy unfair advantages over other departments (as is frequently the case in the humanities) that do not, but may serve the mission of the university equally well? Will my interest in continuing employment as an outside consultant or my ownership in an outside company conflict with—or appear to conflict with—one's roles at the university (AAUP, 1990a, 2013)?

If you are using federal grants or partnering with private industry, you would be well advised to be familiar with the AAUP documents and others that delineate conflicts of interest that might have been produced by professional associations affiliated with your academic discipline. Additionally, it is important for university campuses to develop procedures for disclosing legitimate conflicts of interest, although these should not "improperly interfere with the privacy rights of faculty members and their families" (AAUP, 2013, para. 7). Ultimately, "Because the central business of the university remains teaching and research unfettered by extra-university dictates, faculties should ensure that any cooperative venture between members of the faculty and outside agencies, whether public or private, respects the primacy of the university's principal mission" (AAUP, 2013, para. 6).

Additionally, the AAUP (1990a) describes special situations in government-sponsored research that can arise, including when the faculty member's research may "serve the research or other needs of the private firm without disclosure" (p. 182); "purchase of major equipment . . . for university research from the private firm," (p. 182); "the transmission to the private firm or other use for personal gain of government-sponsored work products, results, materials, records, or information that are not made generally available" (p. 183); "the use for personal gain or unauthorized use of privileged information" (p. 183); "the negotiation or influence upon the negotiation of contracts" (p. 183); and "the acceptance of gratuities of special favors" (p. 183). Further AAUP (1990a) describes potentially problematic areas related to how the faculty member actually spends the amount of time or effort on collaboration with a governmental agency. AAUP also mentions that a faculty member consulting with a governmental agency may also be subject to "conflict of interest provisions in the Federal Criminal Code (18 U.S.C. Sec. et seq.) and the conflict of interest regulations adopted by the National Institutes of Health, the Public Health Service, and the National Science Foundation" (p. 183). Furthermore, there may be state-level regulations as well.

Finally, AAUP advises that the college or university needs to make clear and transparent its accounting procedures and to provide advice to faculty members seeking information about joint ventures that might involve potential conflicts of interest.

Intellectual Property

The recent proliferation of technological innovations raises the issue of to whom do faculty members' creative contributions belong—to the members themselves or to the college or university that employs them. This issue even includes the ownership of online courses. Further, the matter can be complicated by joint ventures with outside agencies, such as with private industry or government agencies. A faculty member's first and best source of guidance is the particular institution's policies obtainable from their technology transfer office or legal counsel that specializes in intellectual property regulations.

If you are completely unfamiliar with notions of intellectual property, you might usefully learn what is meant by such terms as intellectual property, patents, trademarks, copyrights, and trade secrets. According to the World Intellectual Property Organization, the term intellectual property

> refers to creations of the mind: inventions, literary and artistic works, and symbols, names, images, and designs used in commerce. IP is divided into two categories: Industrial property includes patents for inventions, trademarks, industrial designs and geographic indications. Copyright covers literary works (such as novels, poems and plays), films, music, artistic works (e.g., drawings, paintings, photographs and sculptures) and architectural designs (WIPO, n.d. b, p. 3).

Patents protect designs or inventions, such as the design of a specific kind of semiconductor. Trademarks are logos associated with a particular product or organization. Copyrights protect or restrict the use of created or written products. Trade secrets consist of information about the construction or distribution of a product that the controllers of the product do not want unauthorized people to discover.

The WIPO (n.d. a) booklet *Guidelines on Developing Intellectual Property Policy for Universities and R&D Organizations* reviews potential issues that universities and faculty should consider in making determinations about intellectual property ownership, disclosures and partnerships with outside organizations. For example, when embarking on a new creative work you find out answers to such questions as:

- Who owns your intellectual property and any copyrights or patents and earnings that derive from it? Is the owner you, you-and-the-university (or several universities if you have collaborators at other institutions), you-and-some-combination involving the university or a research-and-development company that has partnered with you or a governmental agency that has provided a grant for your research?
- How do you register your patent or disclose your discovery?
- How does the institution balance the academic need for sharing knowledge with trade secrets that are necessary in some areas, such as in military-defense-related work or other governmental project that—according to WIPO—might be sensitive?

Since we do not offer legal advice about specific cases, we recommend that you make contact with your university's technology transfer office or seek out an attorney specializing in this area, or—at the minimum—learn your institution's policies which may be available on a website.

Copyright and Fair Use

This is another area that has received a great deal of attention in academic contexts and is worth considering as options for reproducing materials have increased so substantially, due to technological innovations and the Internet. For distributing copies and creating course packs (compilations of readings from various sources), you would be well advised to consult university library resources on fair use, such as Stanford University Libraries (2014). Such sites will explain how to obtain permission from publishers to include material in course packs. Your professional copy shop or university bookstore to which you submit your work may do this (but you should inquire) or you might have to do it yourself. Please note that it is not permissible to reproduce large sections of textbooks in lieu of actual textbook purchase. Handing out a copy of an article or poem for a class may be permissible in some circumstances for educational purposes, but you need to determine this under current fair use policies. Alternatively, you may be able to direct students to appropriate websites where they can view materials themselves, or work with an academic publisher who will compile a unique textbook for your classes consisting of selected chapters or readings from various textbooks for which the publisher holds copyright into a single text with a unique ISBN. Even reproducing links to material might be protected by law. Further, because something is available on-line or freely available does not mean that it is not protected by copyright.

Another area that may be important to consider is whether it is permissible to show copyrighted diagrams/pictures/videos to classes or as part of Powerpoint or other presentations. This may be of particular interest to those teaching in the arts and music. Because this is a complex area of law where many changes in case law occur, especially considering technological advances and unique scenarios (and because we do not provide legal advice), we recommend that you consult with appropriate university staff members trained in this area and knowledgeable about your individual needs and circumstances.

Other Ethical and Legal Considerations

In addition to the previously described areas and to ethical guidelines proposed by major associations in your field, there are other ethical topics about which we would hope most new professors would be knowledgeable but may not be. In preparation for this chapter, the first author interviewed the associate executive director of the University of Hawai'i Professional Assembly (the faculty union), Kristeen Hanselman on April 19, 2012. One of the charges of the union is to handle grievances, and to represent faculty members who have had accusations of misconduct leveled at them or are involved in other grievances. Given that she has this background, we asked her what advice she would have for new faculty members, to keep themselves out of trouble. She had five major recommendations, which we paraphrase and elaborate on below:

1. Understand ethical practices and scholarship. Specifically, know appropriate uses of grant moneys. This can relate to conflicts of interest, described earlier, such as not using equipment purchased through a grant for an outside business.
2. Know appropriate policies on email, technology, and uses of university equipment. Your university email account can be tracked by the university and may be owned by the university, or the state. It should not be used for inappropriate or non-university business.
3. Know appropriate policies and preventative measures regarding workplace violence and harassment. The majority of cases with which she is familiar are between faculty members, but some also involve faculty and students.
4. Don't date, touch, sext, send provocative tweets or make provocative comments to students. Interactions like these establish a record and can be construed as sexual overtures even if not intended as such.
5. Document events. Always keep records of what happened and when it occurred (e.g., a conflict with a student or another faculty member or another event that you believe merits documentation). Make sure to document as closely as you can to the time the event occurs, as your recollection will deteriorate. According to Hanselman (2012), accurate documentation has saved many faculty members when disputes have arisen.

In addition to Hanselman's (2012) suggestions, we add that you should not pursue romantic or sexual liaisons with students, particularly with those for whom you serve in a supervisory capacity. All institutions of higher education in the United States should have explicit policies about sexual harassment specifically and harassment in general. The misuse of authority and exploitation of students are clearly denounced by the AAUP (1990b) as inconsistent with academic freedom. Furthermore, we note that harassment/intimidation in the broader context of AAUP's position is not limited to that of a sexual nature and can include religion, ethnicity/culture, political interests, or disability. Thus, harassment or intimidation of any nature should not be tolerated.

CONCLUSION

The intent of this chapter has not been to provide legal advice, but rather to identify a number of issues related to ethics and to suggest resources that we believe can be helpful to faculty members. You may find it useful to obtain copies of your university's legal/ethical guidelines, consult with your institution's legal counsel, and consult with an attorney specializing in this area of law.

TEN

Professorial Politics

The word politics is used throughout this chapter to mean the exertion of power or influence between people. Such power is revealed by the extent to which the behavior of one person or group alters the behavior of another person or group. If Person A's behavior is affected at all by the presence or behavior of Person B, then Person B has some power over Person A. However, if B's behavior has no effect on A's behavior, then B has no power over A. Power frequently is reciprocal, with A and B mutually effecting each other's actions.

The expression *professorial politics* refers to the critically important power relationships among the inhabitants of higher education institutions—administrators, faculty members, support staff, and students. Life in academia is also affected by power exerted by people on the periphery of college and university life—alumni, parents, and donors of funds.

In this chapter we view politics in academia from four perspectives: (a) sources of power, (b) a model of political interaction, (c) illustrative cases, and (d) suggestions for new appointees.

SOURCES OF POWER

In higher education settings, professors' power can derive from various sources, including: authority, professorial rank, scholarly reputation, teaching skill, grant generating skill, academic specialization, argumentative style, types of service, friendship patterns, family connections, and sexual attraction.

First, consider authority as "officially assigned power." Each position in a college or university is accompanied by a particular kind and amount of power over certain other people. That power is either specified in print or understood by dint of custom. People with obvious assigned power are department chairs, deans, provosts, chancellors, presidents, and the like. Furthermore, faculty members who serve on critical committees—such as promotion committees—enjoy ipso facto authoritative power. Conflict arises if the assigned authority and the intended recipient (lecturer, professor, teaching assistant, department secretary, student) do not agree that the person with supposed authority has jurisdiction over the issue at hand.

Next, consider professorial rank. The higher the rank or the longer an individual's time of service (seniority), the greater power over people of lesser rank or service. For instance, faculty members who do not have tenure (instructors, lecturers, assistant professors, visiting professors) have less power than tenured faculty, particularly because tenured members vote on lower ranking members at times of promotion and salary (merit) increases.

Scholarly reputation is a key source of faculty members' power, because colleges and universities derive much of their eminence from their professors' academic fame. Institutions compete for renowned scholars and often go to great lengths to keep such individuals on their faculty. An important source of administrators' and faculty members' judgments of their fellow professors' scholarly accomplishments is the record that a professor presents at the time a tenure or promotion decision is due. On that occasion, fellow department members, promotion committees, and administrators review each candidate's record of research and creative activity. The record not only lists the individual's publications, performances, and products, but often includes the publications themselves (books, journal articles) as well as judgments of the significance of the work in the form of book reviews, awards, prizes, and letters from prominent people in the candidate's domain of expertise. Professors with an exemplary record of scholarly production have greater power than ones with less impressive histories.

A reputation of excellence as a teacher also contributes to a faculty member's power. However, the task of discovering the quality of a professor's teaching is usually quite difficult. Reports of students' anonymous evaluations of teachers can be useful but are far from flawless, especially because an instructor who is a fine teacher for one kind of student may not be effective for another kind.

Over the past half-century or so, the power associated with fund-raising skill appears to have increased, particularly as public monies for higher education have failed to keep up with the cost of operating colleges. Hence, institutions have placed increased value on faculty members who are "good grant writers"—skilled at convincing philanthropic foundations, industries, government agencies, and wealthy individuals to fund higher education projects.

College departments usually are named for the academic disciplines in which the faculty members specialize, such as chemistry, computer science, sociology, geology, religious studies, Slavic languages, anthropology, and the like. The people who inhabit higher education institutions do not assign the same level of prestige or respectability to all disciplines. Some departments are considered more "honorable" than others. Although the status of different disciplines may vary somewhat from one campus to another, and from one person's opinion to another's, there appears to be some general agreement across the nation's higher education institutions about the esteem in which different departments are held. For instance, biological science is likely considered more prestigious than communications, physics is higher than civil engineering, psychology more respected than education, economics finer than physical education, and classics (Greek and Latin) more revered than industrial arts. As a result, in the interaction between faculty members from different departments, professors from more prestigious disciplines may enjoy a power advantage over professors from less prestigious departments.

The phrase argumentative style concerns differences between individuals in their ability and willingness to engage in arguments. Some faculty members seek to avoid confrontations with others, particularly in public settings, such as faculty meetings or before a group of students. Other faculty members seem to relish such clashes. Furthermore, some are more adept than others in spontaneously mounting a line of convincing reasoning. Hence, some differences in power among faculty members result from individuals' argumentative styles.

As explained in chapter 3, service to one's college, profession, and community is one of the three responsibilities expected of most professors (with teaching and research/creative activities being the other two).

To be known as a willing, dedicated, and efficient servant can enhance a person's power.

Faculty members' friendship patterns can significantly affect the influence that individuals wield in professorial politics. As a social organization, a sizable academic department or college can be viewed as a country that consists of fiefdoms, with each fiefdom ruled by a lord who enjoys the support of such followers as other professors (usually of lower rank), instructors, teaching assistants, research assistants, graduate students, and secretaries. Some faculty members are not allied with any fiefdom and thereby operate on their own. There is often competition among fiefdoms, with alliances formed among them to confront particular issues that arise, such as the assignment of offices and research facilities, the election of a department chair, the support of a candidate for promotion, budget allocations, or the assignment of support staff (secretaries, computer technicians, teaching assistants).

Family connections (nepotism)—such as a wife and husband in the same department or an uncle as a dean and his nephew as a professor—can have power implications when such a pair support each other in decision situations.

Likewise, sexual attraction—as between two faculty members, a lecturer and an administrative assistant, or a professor and a student—can also yield power consequences if one of the pair receives favors from the other that interfere with the proper operation of the educational program.

In summary, professorial politics significantly impact the conduct of higher education and affect the fate of faculty members.

A MODEL OF POLITICAL INTERACTION

We find it useful to adopt a framework for interpreting political events in academia. Such a framework or model serves as a lens that emphasizes certain features in political confrontations, casting those features in high relief. The following model is such a scheme that we generated for interpreting the cases of professorial politics that are analyzed later in the chapter.

There are three main components of the model:

1. The aspect of academic life.
2. The political event.

3. The analysis, which focuses particularly on the participants' (a) roles, (b) aims-and-motives, (c) sources of power, and (d) strategies.

In other words:

1. The description of a case begins with the main aspect or realm of academic life that was the setting or issue at stake in the political confrontation, such aspects as professors' salaries, professors' reputations, promotion, tenure, student-faculty relationships, control over facilities, nepotism, and more.
2. Next is the event—a description of what occurred in a political confrontation (who did what, how, when, where) and the outcome of the event.
3. Third is the analysis that explains participants' roles, their apparent aims and motives, sources of power, strategies attempted to achieve their aims, and how their amount-and kind of power compared with that of their opponents.

The term *roles* refers to participants'—either individuals or groups—positions in academia. Aims and motives are the reasons behind an individual's or group's seeking to defeat another individual or group in a power struggle. Sources of power include the types described earlier in this chapter, such as assigned authority, academic rank, tenure status, reputation as a teacher, and the like. Strategies are the methods participants adopt for gaining advantage over their rivals.

Illustrative Cases

The following section consists of five cases of political events in American higher education institutions. Each case has been chosen to portray a particular arena in which issues of power are apt to occur. It should be apparent that the five represent only a few of the aspects that can involve power struggles. Thus, the five are no more than a miniscule sample of political life in academia.

The following examples are fictionalized and are based on no specific actual events (with the exception of the last example involving class sizes) although these examples are developed to illustrate typical kinds of power struggles in academia.

Case 1: Coping with Nepotism

The Aspect

The word nepotism is commonly defined as "favoritism given to relatives." In higher education, the form of nepotism that has most concerned administrators and faculty members has involved two members of a family holding administrative or professorial positions in the same institution or—especially worrisome—in the same department. The members could be either from the nuclear family (husband/wife, father/daughter) or from the extended family (aunt/nephew, cousin/cousin). The primary concern has been political—the notion that the pair would represent a coalition that, in matters of voting, would usually represent a double vote compared to the single vote cast by other department members. One of the pair might also engage in maneuvers to give the relative special advantages, such as a distinguished scholar pressing for the promotion of a favorite niece who is of questionable competence. And if desirable teaching positions at a prominent college are at a premium, then candidates for a position may not have a fair chance for a job if they are in competition with a relative of the provost, dean, or department chairperson. Particularly in times of financial stress when teaching jobs are hard to find, critics may complain that two members of the same family are getting more than the family's fair share of the college's funds.

As a result of such conditions, higher education institutions have often established hiring policies to prevent nepotism. This typically has meant that relatives could not be hired to teach in the same college, and certainly not in the same department. And if a couple of single professors married while on the faculty, one of them would need to resign.

However, over the past half-century, nepotism rules have not only been relaxed but, in many places, have been eliminated. A principal cause for this change has been the difficulty institutions encountered with attracting or keeping stellar faculty members who insisted on having their spouse hired as well. The trend accelerated across the decades as more women earned advanced degrees and achieved eminence as teachers and scholars. The trend began with universities granting "a few exceptions" when they yearned to hire prominent scholars who would not accept a position unless their mates were appointed as well. Then the nepotism rules themselves eroded.

However, even though family members can increasingly work in the same institution or department, concerns about nepotism continue and are often reflected in recent regulations. For example, the College of Engineering at Ohio State University issued the following policy governing the hiring of new faculty and staff:

> Members of the same immediate family, as well as domestic partnerships, whose qualifications rank each of them first for the positions under consideration may be employed (full-time or a part-time), so long as neither family member is immediately responsible for the decision to hire, or the supervision, direction, evaluation, or salary recommendation of the other. In such instances, all final decisions will be referred to the Office of Academic Affairs for faculty, and to the Office of Human Resources, Organization and Human Resource Consulting, for staff. The College of Engineering requires that an Engineering Nepotism Checklist be on file for every employee in the college. (Ohio State University College of Engineering, 2014)

The Event

Five years ago, during an economic downturn, a state university in New England hired a provost, a woman known for her skill at cutting budgets. To attract her, university officials were obliged to appoint her husband to an assistant professorship in the Department of English. In this department, part-time lecturers taught many high-demand required introductory courses. The provost, in her second year on campus, cut many of the non-tenured positions, including all of the part-time lecturer positions in the English department. To make up for the lack of instructors for high-demand courses, and to incentivize senior faculty at the higher end of their pay scales to retire, the provost adopted a new policy whereby all non-research-related course reductions for senior faculty would be eliminated. Thus, a number of senior faculty that had been claiming course load reductions due to administrative and other service responsibilities suddenly found themselves with heavy teaching loads involving large introductory courses that they had not taught for years.

Now, four years later, the provost's husband was to be considered for promotion to associate professor and tenure status. The appraisal process began with the seven tenured members of the Department of English reviewing the husband's teaching, research, and service record and then voting on whether he deserved the promotion and tenure. Three of the members voted in favor of the advancement; four voted against it. The department chairperson forwarded the candidate's dossier and a report of the vote to the office of the university's vice president of academic affairs, where a final judgment would be rendered.

Just before the end of the academic year in June, the husband was informed that he would henceforth be an associate professor with tenure.

The Analysis

There were five sets of actors in this drama: (a) the provost, (b) her husband, (c) the four faculty members who voted against the promotion, (d) the three who voted in favor, and (e) the vice president and his staff. Each set had apparent motives/aims, sources of power, and strategies to achieve the aims.

Motives. According to a widespread rumor, the four negative votes were intended as retaliation against the provost for her instructional budget cuts and rulings about senior faculty members' teaching loads, while the three positive votes were either the professors' sincere assessment of the husband's record or else an expression of those voters' friendship with the husband and a desire to stay in the provost's good graces. The husband and provost were apparently motivated by a desire for him to progress professionally and enjoy the money and prestige that accompanied the promotion. The vice president was likely motivated by a need to satisfy the provost so the university would not lose her valued service.

Sources of Power. The department members' official power lay in their status as tenured faculty and their right to vote on the promotion. Their unofficial power could include the way they treated the husband — in either an antagonistic or friendly fashion. The husband's source power consisted of his record (publication, teaching, service), his connection with the provost, and his friendship with tenured members of his department. The provost's power came from her high position in the university's authority structure and her apparent skill in balancing university budgets during a fiscal crisis. The vice president's power came from his even higher position in the authority structure, so he could trump decisions made by anyone lower on the authority ladder.

Strategies. The four department members who voted against the promotion used their ballots for pursuing their aims. In their interactions with the husband, some of them might have openly displayed their dislike for him by either ignoring him or being rude and critical. Or they could have sought to mask their disdain by treating him in a friendly manner so as not to risk retaliation by the provost. The husband could have treated his colleagues with contempt so as to let them know that he felt himself superior to them as a result of his being the provost's spouse, in which case he would be openly inviting his colleagues' ire. But he did not. He recognized that the tenured members of the department would be voting on his promotion, so he tried to be civil, although a bit aloof, in his interactions with them. In addition, he didn't want to work in a social atmosphere of antagonism and suspicion. The provost did nothing overt, but her position of authority served as a tacit strategy in its effect on others in the event. The vice president, from his superior position in the authority hierarchy, could issue his judgment about the promotion without needing to account to anyone lower in the structure for his decision.

Case 2: Seeking a Salary Increase

The Aspect

Higher education institutions vary in their salary policies. Some have publicly published pay schedules. Some have schedules available only to administrators and/or faculty members. Others have no schedules, so that each administrator's or faculty member's income is individually negotiated in private. It is also the case that even in places that have printed schedules, authorities can make exceptions, usually in order to attract administrators or professors of sterling quality that may not have the formal qualifications typically required for high pay—such qualifications as years of service or academic degrees. Or a new appointee's salary on the official schedule may be supplemented with other benefits—free or low-cost housing, funds for research or travel, the use of a university auto, extra office space, an administrative assistant, teaching assistants, a secretary, and the like.

A typical published salary schedule is one from Pasadena City College (one of California's 112 public community colleges), which offers two-year associate-of-arts degrees, but—in the popular effort of junior colleges to become four-year institutions—also offers four-year bachelor degrees in several academic fields. The schedule is based on two factors—academic preparation and years of service. Thus, salaries increase as faculty members compile (a) higher academic degrees, plus additional course work, and (b) more years of teaching.

Faculty members' academic preparation is divided into five classes—Class A through Class E. For example, Class B is for individuals with a master's degree plus eighteen semester credits of further study, or for those with a bachelor's degree plus fifty-four additional credits. Class E is for professors with an earned doctorate from an accredited institution, or:

> following completion of a bachelor's degree, graduation from a three-year program at a professionally oriented institution which is accredited by a recognized professional organization which awards accreditation to institutions of higher education for training in that profession and which institution is approved by the California Community Colleges Chancellor's Office, which degree can be translated to the equivalent of a doctorate. (Pasadena City College, 2007)

The schedule lists the monthly salary for each class and each number of years service. For instance, a Class-A instructor who has taught seven years receives $6,064.44 a month, while a Class-E instructor with seven years' service gets $7,345.66. A Class-B faculty member with thirty-three years' teaching experience earns $9,139.40, whereas a Class-E professor with thirty-three years of teaching receives $10,420.58 per month.

In marked contrast to the Pasadena type of fixed schedule is the pay situation in places that have no published salary information, so that each faculty member's remuneration is negotiated privately with a college administrator. In schools that publish salary schedules, everyone who knows a professor's academic credentials and years of service also knows the professor's income. But in places where salaries are settled in private, individuals tend to be hesitant and guarded about discussing such matters, because discussions can lead to friction among faculty members as some feel aggrieved about being shortchanged in comparison to their colleagues. Administrators often favor private negotiation because it permits them freedom to manipulate the compensation system to suit their preferences. Administrators who engage in private negotiations usually hope faculty members will refrain from revealing their incomes, since discussing salaries can foment unrest and resentment within the professorial community.

The Event

Stephanie, a non-tenure track assistant professor at a prestigious university applied for an advertised tenure-track assistant professorship in the geography department of a private four-year liberal arts college that was known for its high academic standards and its large endowment fund. The college's administrators were sufficiently impressed by Stephanie's credentials to pay her travel and hotel expenses so she could visit the college for an interview. As a result of the interview, she was offered a contract by the dean and was told what her salary would be. She was also promised reimbursement for the expense of moving herself and her family to the college town, but the moving expenses would have to be spent by the end of her second year. This policy would compel Stephanie to undertake the move thereby indicating her intention to become a long-term member of the college community. Stephanie, however, instead commuted several hours by train on days that she was required to teach courses or attend meetings at the college.

The college's geography department was small, consisting of a department chairperson and four professors. The chairperson had been on the faculty for more than a decade. Two positions in the department had recently been vacated, as one professor had retired and the other had resigned to teach elsewhere. Consequently, the geography department was now staffed by the chairperson, Stephanie, two other associate professors, and another assistant professor of two years, Linda.

During their first year on the faculty, Stephanie and Linda became close friends and, on one occasion, shared information about how they had negotiated their salaries with the provost. It thus became clear that Linda's annual income was $3,000 higher than Stephanie's, even though both of them had completed their PhD's in the same year. Consequently, at the outset of their second year on the faculty, Stephanie met with the dean to ask that her salary be increased by $3,000. To bolster her request, she reminded the dean of the prestigious university from which she had come, which in her opinion should increase her value to the department. The dean said that was not possible, and he reminded Stephanie to complete her move to indicate her commitment to her new position.

The meeting with the dean prompted Stephanie to search such publications as the weekly *Chronicle of Higher Education* that included announcements of available college and university teaching posts. One position that she found particularly attractive was at a state university closer to her family's home, so she mailed the dossier of her qualifications to the university and received an invitation to come for an interview. As a result of the interview, she was offered the position at a salary $6,500 higher than her current pay. Armed with this information, she scheduled an appointment with the dean. During their discussion, Stephanie showed the dean the university's offer, but said she would like to stay at the college if she could receive a comparable salary increase. The dean again told Stephanie that was not to be. As a consequence, Stephanie resigned at the end of her second year and accepted the position at the state university closer to her home.

Some months later, in a letter from Linda, Stephanie learned that due to salary compression, the salary of the chairperson of the geography department was only $4,000 higher than Stephanie's own pay when she had been at the college.

The Analysis

The most significant participants in this case were (a) Stephanie, (b) the dean, (c) the geography department chairperson, and (d) Linda.

Motives. Stephanie's dual motive was to increase her income and to receive treatment at least equal to that of the other new assistant professor, Linda. The dean's dual aim likely was to save money for the college and not to be told by a lowly assistant professor how much to pay faculty members. Stephanie later suspected that, if the dean had discussed Stephanie's request for a raise in pay with the department chairperson, the chairperson would not have supported Stephanie's appeal, because the chairperson's own salary after he had been a decade in the department was not much higher than Stephanie's own. It seemed apparent that the chairperson's relatively low salary for a veteran faculty member resulted from his lack of stature as a scholar, for he seemed to be no more than mediocre as a teacher, and he had no record of published research. Linda's motive in telling Stephanie her salary was likely no more than that of engaging in a topic of conversation with a friend who had told her of her own salary; Stephanie did not think Linda was trying to make herself appear superior.

Sources of Power. Initially, Stephanie's source of power was her implied threat of resigning from the college if she did not get the requested salary raise. Then, in her second confrontation with the dean, Stephanie strengthened her initial request by flaunting the job offer from the university near her hometown. The dean's power lay in his position of authority as the college's official salary decision maker. The department chairperson's source of power—if, indeed, the dean had consulted him— was in his position as Stephanie's immediate superior in the college's authority structure, with the opportunity to closely view Stephanie's work.

Strategies. Stephanie's initial strategy was to appeal to the dean's sense of fairness so the dean would award her the same salary as the other new assistant professor, whose qualifications appeared similar to Stephanie's own. Stephanie's subsequent strategy consisted of showing the dean the high value another university placed on Stephanie's services; this display included the threat of Stephanie resigning and thereby depriving the college of her talents. The dean's strategy was to hold fast to his original salary decision, despite the loss of Stephanie's services. The department chairperson's strategy—as Stephanie later imagined it— would have been to portray Stephanie as a faculty member of no great worth, so that Stephanie would not deserve higher pay, and her resignation would not be a serious loss to the college.

Case 3: Using Fiefdoms As Power Instruments

The Aspect

Earlier in this chapter we used the term fiefdom as a label for people or individuals that employ control over others and their resources. We proposed that competing fiefdoms often emerge in colleges and universities, particularly within departments. Fiefdoms can be analyzed in terms of their forms, origins, and sources of power.

Forms. A fiefdom is usually a hierarchy in which the amount of control and power is greatest at the top and descends though decreasing levels of authority to the bottom. The top spot in the structure is occupied either by an individual (in role of chief or boss) or by an oligarchy (often two persons, or at most a few) that shares the ultimate responsibility for the fiefdom's operation.

Members of fiefdoms in higher education institutions can be of various sorts. The chief is sometimes a prestigious scholar whom faculty members and students wish to join as collaborators or disciples. In other cases, the chief is not a renowned scholar but, rather, is a highly ambitious faculty member who seeks to build an empire by attracting financial grants to pay for the fiefdom's facilities and personnel. The kinds of people populating an academic fiefdom can include tenured and non-tenured professors, adjunct professors, lecturers, secretaries, research assistants, teaching assistants, technical specialists (computer technicians, statistical analysts, machinists, artists), consultants, and graduate students.

The population of a fiefdom can be small, such as a single professor, one part-time secretary, and three graduate students working out of the professor's office. Or the fiefdom can be very large, including several tenured professors paid by the university, a number of adjunct professors paid out of grant funds, a half-dozen specialists, several secretaries, and a dozen part-time graduate students. Together, the fiefdom's members may occupy an entire floor of a college building, or perhaps a building of their own.

Origins. There are various ways fiefdoms are established. For example, a professor may gradually acquire followers among faculty members and students. Or a department can emphasize a particular aspect of its academic realm (such an aspect as linear algebra in a mathematics department or paleontology in an anthropology department) by hiring experts in that field who will work together. Or a wealthy donor may fund the establishment of a unit dedicated to a particular specialization (such as a Hindu Studies Center in a department of religion), with the unit employing multiple faculty and staff members.

Sources of Power. Three important sources of a fiefdom's political power can be labeled votes and voices, money, and significance and prestige.

Votes and Voices. When a vote is taken within a department or within a campus-wide academic senate, the greater the number of professors (and particularly tenured professors) who are affiliated with a particular fiefdom, the more votes that will be cast in favor that fiefdom's welfare. For instance, imagine that a chemistry department has nine tenured professors, five of whom are associated in some degree with the department's Pharmacological Research Unit. There is a proposal before the faculty to move the unit out of the main chemistry building and into a set of prefabricated structures. The head of the research unit is against the move. In a secret ballot, the proposal is defeated by a vote of five to four.

Even in matters that are not settled by a formal vote, a fiefdom's verbally fluent and vociferous members can dominate faculty discussions of issues that affect the fiefdom's fate, thereby promoting action that favors the fiefdom. In effect, voices join votes as instruments of political power.

Money. In terms of financial support and governance, higher education institutions can be divided between public and private types.

Public colleges and universities are sponsored by the federal government (such as the U.S. Military Academy at West Point, New York) or state, county, or city governments. Thus, funds to operate public institutions come from three principal sources—(a) the sponsoring government, (b) students' tuition fees, and (c) other contributors, such as philanthropic foundations, businesses, and individuals.

Funds to operate private institutions come from two main sources—(a) from non-government groups (religious denominations, philanthropic foundations, alumni associations) and individual donors, and (b) from student tuition fees.

In addition, both public and private institutions can apply for financial grants from government organizations that need the research and development aid that college and university professors are equipped to provide because of their expertise.

Obviously, colleges have always faced the task of collecting enough money to furnish quality education. To obtain funds, a critical job for administrators in public institutions has been to convince state legislatures, county commissioners, and city councils to furnish enough funds to educate students without having to charge such high tuition fees that only wealthy families can send their youths to college.

The dual funding task of private institutions is to (a) attract donors who will make substantial endowments as well as contributing current operating monies and (b) set tuition fees at a high enough level to finance a quality program but, at the same time, not at a level so high that too few competent students will apply. Traditionally, tuition fees in private institutions have been higher—and often much higher—than in public colleges.

The past four decades have witnessed two accelerating trends in the financing of higher education. First, college costs have risen at a rate substantially higher than the rate of inflation in the general society. Second, the ability of traditional sources of funds to provide money at the same rate as in the past has markedly diminished.

> In 1988, the average tuition and fees for a four-year public university rang in at about $2,800, adjusted for inflation. By 2008, that number had climbed about 130 percent to roughly $6,500 a year, and that doesn't include books or room and board. . . . In 2008 the median income was

$33,000. That means if you adjust for inflation, Americans in the middle actually earned $400 less than they did in 1988. Meanwhile, the amount of federal aid available to individual students also failed to keep up. (Censky, 2011)

States', counties', and cities' incomes have plunged, and many private donors have been unable or unwilling to give as much as in the past. An important consequence of this trend has been that college administrators have increasingly urged professors to obtain grants to finance research and public service activities. The more money a professor attracts, the greater the professor's worth in the opinion of administrators who control resources and opportunities, and the greater the political power the professor enjoys within the institution. A fiefdom with more grant money is more powerful than one with less grant money, other things being equal.

Significance and Prestige. But other things are seldom equal. Thus, a third source of power that interacts with votes and money to determine a fiefdom's power is the significance that people attribute to the results of the fiefdom's efforts. In other words, what did the grant givers get for their money?

In academia there have been grant funded projects that failed to produce the results that were promised—or at least predicted—in the original application for the grant. In some cases the money ran out before there were any results to report. In many other cases the results were insignificant, making little or no contribution to knowledge or social welfare. Critics who appraised such projects would dub them "ill-conceived" or "wasteful" or "off target" or "badly managed." Therefore, fiefdoms that first gained political power by winning grant funds to launch or continue a project can lose power later when the time arrives to judge the cost/benefit outcome of the investment.

The following fictitious case, set in a Midwestern state university, illustrates how the interaction between money and significant results can influence professorial politics.

The Event

In this example, the event is not a single incident but, rather, is a continuing sequence of incidents through which the evolution of two fiefdoms' power in a political science department is traced over a five-year period. We've labeled the fiefdoms Group A and Group B.

Group A. The event began with the chairperson of the political science department expressing her distress about the department's weakness in research related to the Internet and social media. Her solution was to hire from another university a thirty-year-old assistant professor known for his ability to find grant money to support social media related projects. To attract this expert, it was necessary for the department to offer him an associate professorship with tenure.

When the new appointee arrived on campus, he not only brought along three grants that he had held at his previous school, but he was also accompanied by three of his previous support staff members and two graduate students whose salaries had been paid from grants rather than regular university funds. Hence, the nucleus of a fiefdom was immediately in place.

Over the next few years, Group A expanded in grant money, membership, territory, and political power. Two staff members spent nearly half of their time hunting for sources of grants and applying for grants that fit the requirements of grant sources. Not only were more support staff and temporary adjunct professors hired from grant funds (temporary "soft money" rather than "hard money" from the regular permanent university fund sources, such as state tax dollars), but three political science tenured professors were drawn into the group as part-time consultants whose regular salaries were supplemented with soft money. Thus, by the social media expert's third year on campus, the number of people associated with Group A totaled eleven.

As Group A's personnel increased, the fiefdom required more office and laboratory space. The university's administrators were glad to provide the additional territory since it would be paid for by grant money ("overhead"). As a result, several professors and graduate student assistants who were not part of Group A were moved out of their offices to other sections of the building. In addition, two classrooms were converted into Group A laboratories and work spaces.

A further factor that would affect the fiefdom's power was the university's tenure and promotion system. Each professorial level (assistant professor, associate professor, full professor) was accompanied by a significant salary increase. Additionally, each promotion required greater scholarly feats than the previous one. In effect, the slope became steeper as the climber advanced. The social media expert had only been at the associate level for three years, instead of the usual four when he submitted a request to be considered for early promotion to full professor. As a result, his publications and research record were reviewed by several experts in his field at other major universities, then his dossier of accomplishments was reviewed at successive levels of the university's promotion review structure: (a) tenured full professors of the political science department, (b) the department chair, (c) the dean of the college of social sciences, and (d) the campus-wide tenure and promotion committee. These recommendations were then sent to the university president's office where a final judgment was rendered. The early promotion was denied.

Group B. This group would barely qualify as a fiefdom. Over the four-year span, it consisted of a single associate professor and three graduate students with whom she had coauthored several academic journal articles. The professor was known as a theorist. Her field of expertise was political theories and structures. The only grants she had ever sought were ones that enabled her to carry out research abroad, and to hire graduate students to collaborate on summer stipends. Her workstation was her office, where she was periodically joined by one or two of her collaborating doctoral students.

A sudden change in her academic reputation occurred during the third year of this five-year period when her book *Emerging Interpretations of Political Systems* was published. The book was lauded internationally by political scientists and lay readers alike as "a welcome fresh look" and "a tour de force." She received a growing number of invitations to deliver keynote speeches at conferences and colloquia and to write articles for prestigious periodicals. Over the next two years, highly respected academic journals published several of her studies of political structures in various cultures. At the outset of the fifth year, the chair of the political science department suggested that she apply for promotion to full professor. The professor's dossier then traveled the route up the authority hierarchy to the university president's office. In late spring, when promotions were announced, she learned that she was promoted to full professor.

The Analysis

The two promotion decisions in the above narrative (denial of promotion for the head of Group A and advancement for the head of group B) are analyzed here from two perspectives—those of (a) professors on review committees (department, academic senate) and (b) university administrators (department head, dean, president).

First, consider the case of Group A's leader—the social media expert—who applied for early promotion.

Review Committee Professors. Committees of professors at two levels of the authority hierarchy (department and campus-wide tenure and promotion committees) offered opinions about the worthiness of the candidates for promotion.

The Department's Report. The departmental committee was composed of ten political science tenured full professors. We assume that their judgments were based on (a) their appraisal of the candidates' publications (quantity and scholarly quality) (b) the opinions of the external reviewers as experts in the candidate's research area about the quality of the candidates' research, and (c) their personal relationships with the candidates as fellow department members.

In the case of the Group A leader, four professors voted for the promotion and six voted against it. Those who favored the promotion supported their decision with such reasons as:

"He's had several worthwhile publications."
"Was responsible for building a strong social media unit in the department."
"Has brought a great deal of grant funds to the university."
Department members who voted against the promotion appended such comments as:
"Although he's brought in grants, the number and quality of publications should be higher to merit promotion to full professor."
"External reviews are mixed."
"The writing style is often journalistic rather than scientific."
"The evidence isn't convincing enough to warrant promotion to full professor at this time. He should wait."

In addition to department members basing their opinions on such considerations as the above, we suspect that the committee members' personal relations with the head of Group A might also influence their vote. For instance, professors who had received money from the fiefdom would likely look more favorably on the promotion than would professors who had been ousted from their offices or had their usual classrooms converted into the fiefdom's laboratories and workrooms.

The Campus-Wide Tenure and Promotion Committee's Report. The six members of the campus-wide tenure and review committee were drawn from various departments across the campus, such as physics, classics, foreign languages, economics, education, and the like. Their role was to bring standards of scholarship and productivity from their own disciplines to the appraisal of candidates for promotion. They reviewed the assessments of each candidate made by appraisers lower in the authority structure (department committee, department chair, dean), as well as appraisals by the external reviewers (who commented on scholarly quality of research) and added their own evaluation before sending the set of reports to the university president. The tenure and promotion committee's report concluded with the opinion that the head of Group A should not be promoted because:

> "The candidate's scholarly performance fails to represent the quality of scholarship that can reasonably be expected for promotion to professor. While his grantsmanship is laudable, the quality and quantity of research publication appears rather pedestrian, lacking in the novelty, critical insight, or theoretical underpinning that should distinguish the work of a full professor. He would be well-advised to focus on developing his publication record further."

Administrators. We might expect administrators' promotion decisions to be influenced by both money and academic considerations, so that candidates for advancement would be judged on both their skill at attracting grant funds and their scholarship. The department chair, dean, and president would be acutely aware of the need for grant funds to operate the university, particularly as the state was in deep debt, no longer able to finance higher education at past levels. Thus, professors' skill in fund-raising would deserve consideration in matters of promotion. At the same time, administrators (who usually have been, or still are, professors) recognize that the reputation of research universities ultimately depends on the quality of contributions to knowledge and social progress made by scholars. Thus, administrators are obliged to balance scholarship against fund-raising in their promotion decisions. We assume that was true in the case of Group A's leader, so that contributions to knowledge in this case trumped money.

Now to the case of Group B's leader—the political structures theorist—who was promoted to full professor status.

Department Promotions Committee. In preparing the case for appraisal, the chairperson of the political science promotions committee had sent letters to eight distinguished political scientists at other universities, soliciting their opinions of the candidate's publications, and particularly of her most recent book, *Emerging Interpretations of Political Systems*. The eight experts included five in the United States, two in Europe, and the editor of a prominent political science journal. The replies from all eight supported the promotion, referring to the book and recent articles as "brilliantly crafted," "on the frontier," and "full of persuasive insights." The reviews of the book that the chairperson collected from academic journals were equally enthusiastic.

After the department's tenured professors had studied the evidence compiled by the chair (including copies of the candidate's recent publications, students' assessments of her teaching, her record of university service, the eight letters from outside appraisers, and the book reviews), they voted unanimously in favor of promotion to full professor.

University Tenure and Review Committee. The report that the committee forwarded to the university president summarized the evidence in support of the promotion, then concluded with the following paragraph:

> All members of our committee were extremely impressed with the candidate's scholarship. It appears that she has elevated our political science department to a prominent place on the international political theory map. In view of the exceptional quality of her research, teaching and service, we believe that this promotion is well deserved.

Administrators. Both the department head and dean of social sciences had agreed with the department committee's recommended promotion to full professor. Subsequently the decision makers in the university presidents' office were persuaded by the campus-wide faculty committee's report that the promotion candidate's eminent position in her field of expertise warranted her moving to full professor.

Postscript

We have chosen to describe this case in detail in order to introduce the notion of fiefdoms in academia and to illustrate one way that the interaction between grant money and scholarly prestige can affect professors' status in research oriented universities. The grant funds in this case resulted in outcomes that were of service to news media and some academic journals rather than being significant contributions to knowledge that would result in publication in higher tier academic journals or in patents or other intellectual property that might be the case in some other disciplines like biology or chemistry. However, in a great host of research projects in universities, grant funds are vital for the creation of new knowledge and products.

Case 4: Finding the Best Dissertation Committee

Not only are administrators and professors important in campus politics, but students and members of the support staff (secretaries, technicians, custodians, and the like) are also significant players.

The Aspect

An important task faced by doctoral students is that of forming a committee of professors who will serve as advisors for the candidates' dissertation research. It's a task affected by professorial politics.

The Event

At the end of her second year as a doctoral student in the university's communications department, Claire began planning the research project that would result in the dissertation she would write to earn her degree. To learn how to go about the task, she consulted Carlos, a fourth-year student who had just completed his dissertation. Carlos told Claire that she would need to select three professors from the department to serve as her advisers who would guide her research and assess the final product. And she would also need to select two committee members from outside the department. The discussion went rather like this:

Carlos: "Getting the right advisers is a tricky business. You need three from our department who will really help. Getting the wrong combination could make your life very difficult."

Claire: "How do I find them? Ask the department chair?"

Carlos: "No, you'll get better advice from the department's administrative assistant, Louise. She's been in that job for over twenty years. The department chair has been in her job only two years, and in another year or so she'll be replaced, since it's a rotating job. Tell Louise that you're trying to put together a dissertation committee. She knows all about the professors, because so much correspondence and gossip about them passes through her office. She helped me when I was in your situation."

Claire then spoke with Louise:

Louise: "In what field of communications do you intend to do your research?"

Claire: "Intercultural—about communication patterns in childhood and adolescence."

Louise: "Four of the professors are strong in intercultural—Foster, Janish, Smith, and Doloski. Have you had classes with any of them?"

Claire: "Foster, Janish, and Smith."

Louise: "How well did you do in those courses? And how well did you get along with the professors?"

Claire: "I got A's from Janish and Smith—an A-minus from Foster. I liked them well enough. I found Janish friendlier than the others."

Louise: "The problem with Smith is that he's away from campus giving keynotes at conferences and consulting so often that you'd have a hard time getting hold of him when you needed to discuss what you're doing as you move from one stage of the dissertation to another."

Claire: "Then I should have Foster and Janish on the committee?"

Louise: "Well, you might consider how well they work together."

Claire: "Oh, I've heard they've had some confrontations."

Louise: "You don't want faculty members that don't get along. They could disagree about what you do and how you do it. If you think they don't get along you'd better pick one of them."

Claire: "All right. Maybe Janish. But I need three."

Louise: "There's Doloski. He and Janish collaborate on research. Will your dissertation topic involve linguistics?"

Claire: "It might, since it relates to language acquisition, too. I've got several ideas for topics, but I haven't settled on one yet. That's part of why I need a committee."

Mrs. Miller: "Then there's Professor Cohen. She's just an assistant professor, but she's a specialist in linguistic aspects of development. She gets along all right with Doloski and Janish. And then you need to select one of them to chair the committee—to be your main adviser."

Claire: "Which would you suggest?"

Louise: "The highest ranking of the three is Doloski. He has a big international reputation. If there are disagreements among the committee members, he's the one who has enough power to see that the conflict is settled in your favor."

Claire: "So how do I get the three of them to be on the committee?"

Louise: "Make an appointment to see each one so that you can ask if they'll serve. Start with Doloski, and ask if he would be willing to be the chair."

The Analysis

The active participants in this case were the inexperienced graduate student (Claire), the experienced graduate student (Carlos), and the communications department's administrative assistant (Louise). Passive participants were the communications department's professors whose envisioned characteristics influenced the outcome of the case.

Claire's aim was to find the most useful, supportive advisers as possible. Carlos's and Louise's principal motive was altruistic—to help a needy graduate student. Louise and Carlos's motives may well have included self-aggrandizement—an opportunity to display a fund of knowledge about matters of dissertation advisory committees and of professors' attitudes and sources of power.

Claire's strategies in pursuit of her aim involved seeking the advice of knowledgeable acquaintances (Carlos and Louise), whose strategy was that of frankly revealing what they knew about the nature and function of dissertation advisors.

Case 5: Divided Power — Administration, Senate, and Union

The Aspect

As suggested earlier in this chapter, authority is power that is officially assigned to a group or individual.

In private colleges and universities, the top of the authority hierarchy is typically occupied by a board of governors whose members hold distinguished positions in the business world, politics, science, or the arts; or members may simply be individuals who have inherited great wealth and enjoy the power that accompanies riches. Board members are not involved in the day-to-day operation of the institution. Instead, they meet only periodically to set general policies that are to be carried out by the college's top administrators, such as the president or chancellor. Then, at descending steps below the top administrators are provosts, deans, department heads, professors, support staff, and students.

In public higher education institutions, the authority hierarchy is usually more complex than in the private sector. At the top of the power pyramid is the state legislature, which sets regulations that dictate how public schools and colleges are to operate. Those regulations can be rather general or they can be very specific, such as specifying what courses are to be offered and even what topics of study are to be included within a course. The authority levels below the legislature can vary from state to state, but they often descend through a statewide board of education, an office governing public colleges statewide, a board of overseers for each college, and the administrators, teachers, support staff, and students in each college, institute, or university.

Conflicts over power—over who decides what—arise whenever (a) the division of power among the units in an authority hierarchy is not clearly specified, (b) people lower in the hierarchy have greater skill or confidence or ambition than ones above them in the system and thereby attempt to usurp the power of their superiors, or (c) new "players" invade a traditional hierarchy.

The case we will use to illustrate conflicts within a state authority structure involves a struggle over the maximum number of students to be permitted in the classes of a California junior college. To explain why such a matter would become the focus of a power struggle, we need to preface the case with a bit of historical background.

According to Cuesta College professor Peter Dill (personal communication, March 27, 2012), three entities that compete in governing every California public junior college are the college's administration, labor union, and academic senate. Each of these entities acts from the viewpoint of a particular conception or model of governance that derives from the entity's historical roots.

The Administration's Perspective. The origin of public junior colleges in the United States can be traced back to high schools that added a year of school study beyond their normal grade twelve. The focus of the extra year was to provide teacher training for elementary teachers or vocational training, in business, trades, or home economics. Often a second post–high school year was added. Eventually the two years were split from the high school to form a two-year junior college. Thus, the model of governance from elementary and secondary schools was carried into the junior college. Dill labels that form of governance the business model in which ultimate power is held by a board at the top (the district school board) and delegated to the chief operating officer as "the big boss" (superintendent for all schools), and then to lower level administrators (principals of individual schools). Those members of the administration make all important decisions about how schools should operate. Teachers, support staff, and students are obligated to carry out the administration's orders. The typical aim of the administration's business model is to educate the young at the most cost effective level.

The Labor Union's Perspective. The purpose of labor unions is to further the welfare of workers by pressing employers to provide adequate pay and reasonable working conditions. That perspective is the trade union model.

The two main nationwide unions which college employees can join (professors and members of the support staff) are the National Education Association (NEA) and the American Federation of Teachers that is affiliated with the AFL/CIO (American Federation of Labor and Congress of Industrial Organizations). The NEA is the largest union in the United States with more than 3 million members from pre-school educators to university professors (National Education Association, 2014). The American Federation of Teachers has 1.6 million members in over 3,000 local affiliates (American Federation of Teachers — AFL-CIO, 2014).

In California, the trade union model became extremely important when the state legislature in 1975 passed the Rodda Act, a law decreeing that all public school teachers and support staff members—kindergarten through the university—would henceforth become members of a single collective bargaining union, the California Teachers Association. The aim of the Rodda Act was the improvement of personnel management and employee-employer relations in California's public schools by determining how grievances over working conditions and wages would be arbitrated. Unions were also given power over certain specific functions, such as determining qualifications for professors' appointment and promotion (The Rodda Project, 2007). Those powers are specified in written contracts between the union and colleges.

The Academic Senate's Perspective. Over the centuries, as higher education developed in Europe and was transported to the Americas, the governance of colleges was dominated by the professors. They set the rules about how colleges would operate. This practice of having the experts in a profession or craft wielding ultimate power is what Dill identifies as the guild model. Guilds in higher education have consisted of experts in the teaching profession organizing to ensure the quality of their vocational calling. Early in the thirteenth century, such guilds originated among university students in Bologna and among masters (instructors) in Paris and Oxford. Over the centuries, the professorial guild assumed the form of an academic senate, a body whose chief aim is to ensure a high level of scholarship in teaching (equipping learners with knowledge and skills) and in producing new knowledge (research and creative activity). In the 1960s through the 1980s, California legislators and junior college personnel worked to develop academic senates. Thus, what were formerly called junior colleges became "community colleges." No longer considered as extensions of high schools, community colleges would be patterned after four-year colleges, each with a centralized governance structure—an academic senate (Academic Senate for California Community Colleges, 2010).

Such then, is the historical setting in which our class-size event occurred.

The Event

In this case, the event was not a single incident but, rather, was a series of periodic incidents concerning the question of the proper number of students that should be enrolled in a community college class. The issue became a matter of open debate whenever changing conditions brought class size to the forefront of the faculty's attention—such conditions as a drop in state funding for colleges, a new classroom building to be constructed, or instructors of English composition classes complaining of not being able to bear the burden of correcting students' written compositions when so many students were assigned to their classes.

On one such occasion, representatives of the administration, labor union, and academic senate met to consider the administration's proposal that (a) the current maximum class size be raised and (b) classes in which enrollment fell below a given level should be cancelled. The reason given for such a change was that the income from state and county taxes had dropped, making it necessary to serve the same number of students on far fewer funds.

Members of the academic senate objected to the administration's plan and proposed that different standards for class size be set for different types of classes so as to maintain high quality instruction. Classes taught by a traditional lecture method could be larger than ones requiring more personalized supervision of students. Thus, an art appreciation class, utilizing lectures illustrated with projected media in a large auditorium, could be far larger than an industrial welding class or the music department's stringed instrument practicum.

Representatives from the union objected to the administration's proposal from the perspective of what the change would mean for faculty members' working conditions—how burdensome the plan would be for both professors and support personnel (technicians, secretaries, custodians).

The compromise that was reached on this occasion featured the financial concerns of the administration and the union's concern for fairly compensating faculty and staff members (money and vacation time) for the time they spent on the job and for their level of responsibility. The senate's interest in maintaining high quality instruction was given less weight in the compromise than either the administration's position or the union's position.

The Analysis

The dominant aims of the three groups in the class size negotiations derived from each group's dominant perspective—the administration's business model, the labor union's model, and the academic senate's model.

The main strategy attempted by representatives of all three parties was that of logical argument—each group's portrayal of positive outcomes of its own perspective and of disastrous results of the other two contending groups' proposals. The administration's claim of financial disaster was bolstered by the undeniable facts of the current economic recession. The union's position in the debate was supported by the fact that in the Rodda Act of 1975, the California Teachers Association had been given authority over issues that bore on faculty compensation and working conditions. The academic senate—although able to argue persuasively about the effect of class size on quality of instruction—lacked the union's authority as mandated in the Rodda Act. In effect, official authority trumped instructional quality pleas.

Finally, we wish to suggest an implication this case holds for graduate students who are hunting for a college teaching position. When you investigate institutions to decide whether you would like to teach there, you may find it useful to learn if the college has a labor union. And if it does, you might profit from reading the union's contract to discover what facets of a professor's life are affected by the types of authority assigned to the union as compared to the types assigned to the administration and senate.

SUGGESTIONS FOR NEW APPOINTEES

While in no way can we anticipate fully the political situations that you, as a newly appointed college teacher, may find yourself in, we have some general suggestions about how you might cope with the political aspects of your position.

- Analyze your department in terms of alliances, fiefdoms, and power struggles. Where do you most naturally see yourself fitting in? Perhaps you will fit in with others who share similar research or academic interests. Perhaps, too, you will gravitate toward other newer or untenured faculty members.
- Remember that these people are your colleagues, not your personal friends. Personal friends are those with whom you discuss family matters, relationship difficulties, health issues, and interpersonal gossip. Professors who exhibit professionalism keep these areas

separate from work. So it's best to keep your personal social life separate from your work life. While we are not suggesting that you do not socialize with your colleagues, your colleagues make a very risky close interpersonal friendship (and dating!) pool. Remember that when you break up with an intimate friend you might be compelled to face this person every work day for the next ten or twenty years. Also, close interpersonal ties can interfere with objective decision-making in tenure and promotion evaluations, requiring persons to excuse themselves from such tasks.

- Do participate in departmental gatherings and social events, but remember, these are work-related events and not the time to drink a few too many.
- Try to not ally yourself with one fiefdom or camp at the expense of alienating other groups or faculty members if there is some sort of departmental struggle. Remember that the group that appears to be "on top" today might be outmoded tomorrow. Furthermore, faculty members retire or find positions elsewhere as years go by and departments reorganize, so the political terrain might change significantly.
- Find a mentor (either formally through a mentoring program or informally through interpersonal connections) outside of your department who is knowledgeable about university politics and can give you an outside-of-the-department perspective and advice.
- If you find yourself in a "minority position" in your department by virtue of your ethnicity, gender, sexual orientation, research interest, or the like, try to find support outside of the department so as to create your own positive social network.

CONCLUSION

Our purpose in this chapter has been to suggest the importance of power relationships in higher education institutions by identifying sources of political power and by illustrating varieties of power confrontations found in colleges, institutes, and universities.

ELEVEN

Promotion and Tenure

When you have heard about tenure and promotion, you may have expected them to be separate processes and then have wondered how such processes might impact you as a faculty member. In this section, we explain those two terms and their origins and provide suggestions that might help you succeed as you plan for tenure and promotion.

TENURE'S ORIGIN

The concept of tenure derives from the Latin verb tenere, meaning to hold. The term tenure was first used to refer to land-tenure systems in the Middle Ages.

In the 1920s in the United States, an effort was made to make professors' positions more permanent and to counteract college trustees' negative decisions about faculty members whose research findings or whose political or philosophical positions differed with the trustees' own. The importance of academic freedom—the freedom to pursue one's research and teaching truthfully without feeling pressured to compromise—was considered to be central to professors' roles in public institutions of higher learning and hence is very closely tied to the rationale for tenure. A view of the need for academic freedom—and tenure—is expressed in the following Statement of Principles on Academic Freedom and Tenure by the American Association of University Professors (1940):

1. Teachers are entitled to full freedom in research and in the publication of the results, subject to the adequate performance of their

161

other academic duties; but research for pecuniary return should be based upon an understanding with the authorities of the institution.

2. Teachers are entitled to freedom in the classroom in discussing their subject, but they should be careful not to introduce into their teaching controversial matter which has no relation to their subject. Limitations of academic freedom because of religious or other aims of the institution should be clearly stated in writing at the time of the appointment.

3. College and university professors are citizens, members of a learned profession, and officers of an educational institution. When they speak or write as citizens, they should be free from institutional censorship or discipline, but their special position in the community imposes special obligations. As scholars and educational officers, they should remember that the public may judge their profession and institution by their utterances. Hence they should exercise appropriate restraint, should show respect for the opinions of others, and should make every effort to indicate that they are not speaking for the institution. (AAUP, 1940. Reprinted with permission from the American Association of University Professors)

TENURE POLICIES IN PRACTICE

As explained in chapter 3, many educators at two-year and four-year institutions in the United States are identified as assistant professors, associate professors, or full professors. An assistant professor typically has a doctoral degree—or at least a master's degree—in his or her field of expertise and is hired shortly after earning the degree, or perhaps after having served as a post-doctoral fellow in a research position for one to three years after graduating.

New appointees are usually hired as assistant professors without being awarded tenure status and must serve a probationary period (typically five or six years), after which they apply for advance to tenure and promotion to associate professor. The process of applying for tenure and promotion involves documenting one's contributions in teaching, research, and service. The document that the candidate prepares—often referred to as a dossier—is reviewed by the chairperson of the individual's department, by tenured department members (often in the form of a committee of selected members), by one's dean, by a university-wide committee, by other administrators, and by external reviewers, who are usually professors in other colleges and universities. Each reviewer analyzes the contents of the dossier and offers an opinion about whether or not the applicant should be elevated to tenure status. Among external reviewers, the most critical evidence in the dossier for faculty members in a research university is the candidate's scholarly contributions in the form of research, public performances, and products.

After recommendations from the candidate's department and external reviewers have been compiled, the appraisal process usually advances to the academic dean of the college and then to a university-wide promotion committee composed of representatives from various departments who offer their own analyses of the case. Finally, the reports compiled from each of these bodies are sent to the office of the college or university president where a final judgment is rendered about tenure and promotion. If tenure is denied, the candidate may be retained on the faculty for one more year, but then will be dismissed.

After a successfully promoted associate professor has served at that level for a certain number of years (with the number depending on the particular institution's policy), she or he can apply for promotion to full professor, with the expectation that the individual will thereafter perform even greater feats of research, teaching, and service.

SUGGESTIONS FOR TENURE AND PROMOTION PLANNING

If you are hired in a tenure-track position, you will need to begin planning for the process of tenure and promotion from the time you first join the faculty. Following are suggestions that might help you succeed in the process:

- Contact your department chairperson to obtain a copy of your department's guidelines for tenure and promotion. Usually, research productivity is primary among "what counts" for the tenure process in research institutions, although this may be variable, depending upon whether you are employed at an institution that highly values research or teaching, or some combination of both. How many refereed journal articles or performances or books are expected of you? Of what quality? Are external grants valued? What kinds of grants, from what sorts of institutions, and for what amounts? When are you expected to apply for tenure and promotion? Ask for samples of successful dossiers to use as models.

- Plan a research, performance, or product agenda before you begin your first faculty position. Most new professors' first publications are derived from their dissertation research. Recognize that it takes time to have journal articles accepted for publication. It's not uncommon for the review process to take several months. You may well receive several rejections before you find the right journal. For example, one assistant professor published what he considered to be several smaller research papers first and then published the article based on his dissertation after he was tenured. It is often better to expend your energy on several projects than to focus on only one.

- Keep your curriculum vitae up-to-date, with categories clearly delineating journal articles, book chapters, conference presentations, service to the profession, university, college, department, and community. You should clearly differentiate refereed from non-refereed publications and presentations. Otherwise, reviewers of your case may suspect that you are attempting to "pad" your CV. As soon as you have presented a paper at a professional conference or had a paper accepted for publication, list it in your CV.

- Keep a separate listing of all committees on which you serve, adding a note about the role you assume on the committee.

- If your teaching has been formally evaluated by students in your classes, you can summarize the results (such as percentages or averages). You may choose to have someone else prepare the report—thereby adding to the credibility of the evaluation process—rather than preparing it yourself.

- Invite senior faculty members or other colleagues to observe your teaching. Ask them to write memos regarding their experience, and save these for inclusion in your dossier. You might do this every year or semester to show your performance consistency or to demonstrate improvement.

- Your department might require annual contract renewals each year before you apply for tenure and promotion. You may find it useful to write a draft of the type of document you'll use in the formal tenure application so that you can obtain colleagues' feedback during the year before you actually do apply for tenure and promotion.

If your department or department chairperson conducts annual reviews of professors' performance that include suggestions for ways to improve in the future, your next application for promotion may profitably include ways that you have applied those suggestions. If your department does not voluntarily summarize your annual review in writing, you might write an email to your department chair summarizing the main points of the discussion (i.e., your areas of accomplishment and suggestions for improvement or further focus). Ask if he or she concurs that this is an accurate summary of the discussion. Retain this documentation in case you might need it later.

- If you are required to put together a narrative describing your work as part of your tenure dossier, you will generally write about your accomplishments in research, teaching, and service. Have someone outside your field read your narrative to make sure it's comprehensible to non-experts. Explain why your work is valuable; and in some fields, it's helpful to explain why your work is valuable to different audiences. For example, in the field of professional education, some publications are aimed toward a readership of teachers, others toward academics. You might also explain how solely authored versus multiple-authored publications are regarded in your field. In the social sciences, most academics have some sole-authored and some shared authorship articles, while in a science like physics it is common to see a listing of many authors for a single publication. Finally, it might be important to explain what is valued in your discipline. For example, if you are in an art department, displaying your work in a highly regarded juried exhibit might be very important. If you are in a computer science department, publication of some refereed conference proceedings might be valued almost as highly as refereed journal articles, due to the speed at which innovation takes place, whereas conference proceedings might be much less valued in a sociology department. Lastly, if you are in a unique work position—librarian, research specialist, or have a joint appointment in two or more departments—you may need to explain exactly what your duties are so that others can clearly see whether you have fulfilled them.
- If you are required to write an extended narrative, you might examine departmental and university strategic planning documents and

describe how your work advances these goals. For many professors, proposing the importance of their work sounds like bragging and is thus uncomfortable. But it's important that you be forthright about how significant your contributions are.

- If your department does not require an extended narrative, focus on making sure your list of publications, conference contributions, and other contributions is complete.

- In your dossier, it is imprudent to identify what you think are your shortcomings or limitations. Perhaps your teaching evaluations have become more positive with time. This is expected, because many new faculty members have limited or no teaching experience. It is enough to describe how you have grown to be more effective as an instructor and document how you have done that, so it is important to highlight your positive accomplishments.

- Keep files for each of the three areas—teaching, research, and service. Whenever you receive a letter of thanks or other appropriate documentation (including letters and emails from former students), select the best for inclusion in appendices to your dossier along with positive opinions of your work that have been written by journal editors and reviewers.

- Identify who your publication collaborators are (e.g., senior faculty, graduate students that you have mentored). In most situations, it is prudent to limit your collaborations on publications with senior faculty members, such as your dissertation advisor so as to establish your independence as a researcher. On the other hand, your department may value collaborative grants with other departments or universities. You may wish to ask what kinds of collaborations are most valued in your academic specialization and your department.

- Keep track of your national and international research colleagues whom you meet through conferences and professional journals. You might be asked to submit names of people in your field to act as external reviewers of your work. You may not feel comfortable asking such people to serve as external reviewers (in fact, you might be required to not ask them yourself, as their evaluations of your research will likely be solicited by your department and confidential), but it helps to have made contact with more senior faculty members at other institutions who are in your research area and are interested in your research progress, as you might be in theirs as well.

- Early on, as we mentioned in the previous chapter, find a mentor, such as a senior faculty member, whom you can consult if you have questions about departmental politics and procedures. Sometimes universities have faculty-mentoring programs through which you could find a mentor or mentorship group.

CONCLUSION

As described in this chapter, most faculty members in tenure-track positions are required to apply for promotion and tenure after five to seven years in their positions. They typically create dossiers that delineate their accomplishments in the areas of teaching, research, and service. Reprints of a professor's research articles will be sent out for evaluation to confidential reviewers in the applicant's research area, with the reviewers then proposing whether the quality and productivity of the applicant would merit promotion and/or tenure at their own institutions. Dossiers and confidential reviewer letters are then evaluated by departments, department chairs, deans, university-wide faculty committees, and higher level administrators, such as university vice chancellors. These decision-makers will determine whether a faculty member merits promotion to the next higher level—as either an associate professor or full professor—and whether the applicant merits tenure and a promise of continuing employment.

IV

Postscript

TWELVE

The Future

Careers in Higher Education

In this final chapter, we attempt to (a) predict conditions in higher education in the years ahead and (b) estimate what implications those conditions hold for graduate students and others who contemplate a career in college teaching. Our speculation about the future is founded on the assumption that trends in higher education institutions during recent years will continue at least through the coming decade and probably beyond.

THE YEARS AHEAD

The topics addressed in the following pages include: (a) financing higher education, (b) kinds of institutions, (c) kinds of jobs, and (d) methods of instruction.

Financing Higher Education

We begin with the funding of colleges and universities because all of the other matters discussed in this book are affected by the availability of money. Recent trends in students' college costs are likely harbingers of difficult times for students and their families in the future. Consider, for example, the rise in the price of a college education over the past three decades. According to the National Center for Education Statistics (2012),

171

between 1980–1981 and 2010–2011, a student's average annual cost at a public four-year institution rose from $2,550 to $15,918 and at a public two-year college grew from $2,027 to $8,085. At private four-year institutions, a student's average annual expense in 1980 was $5,594 and by 2010–2011 was $32,617, while in two-year private colleges the cost rose from $4,303 to $23,871.

> Since 1982 a typical family income increased by 147 percent, more than inflation but significantly behind the huge increase in college costs. College costs have been rising roughly at a rate of 7 percent per year for decades. Since 1985, the overall consumer price index has risen 115 percent while the college education inflation rate has risen nearly 500 percent. . . . Blunting these increases is a rise in federal student aid including tax credits and deductions. And nearly two thirds of undergraduates now receive some sort of grant aid and student loan borrowing is on the upswing. But loans must be paid back so the pain of payment is only delayed. (Odland, 2012, para. 4)

There is no sign that such a rapid rise in costs will change in years to come. Next, consider trends in the expense of operating colleges and universities and in the sources of those institutions' incomes. In recent years, higher education's financial condition has been bleak not only for students but also for the people who operate colleges and universities—administrators, faculty, and staff.

At the same time that continuing inflation has raised institutions' costs, public tax monies for education have declined in most states and communities. Not only have public funds diminished, but higher education has had to compete with other publicly funded services for the available money such as Medicaid (Katsinas, Buchholz, Priest, Palmer, and Tollefson, 2004). As noted by Nancy McCallin, director of the Colorado public junior-college system, "Over 600,000 Coloradans are on Medicaid right now . . . and so [lawmakers] view higher education in the state legislature as one of the places they can cut partially because they think we can offset it with increased tuition" (McCallin in Cotton, 2012, para. 18).

> Unfortunately, what you are seeing in Colorado is that because state funding has gone down most recently from $706 million to a little under $500 million for state institutions, there's been a switch, and what happens is that when state funding goes down, some of the cost of public education is going on to the student. About five years ago approximately 60–70 percent for the funding of higher education was

coming from the state. Today that is flipped: 60–70 percent is coming from the student. (McCallin in Cotton, 2012, para. 13)

Specifically, Cotton (2012) describes an increased enrollment in universities and colleges during the years 2007–2008 and concomitant decreases in state funds by 31 percent or $216 million in 2010–2012. Although other states have been in similar predicaments, some states have been able to increase state funding, such as Montana, up by 18 percent and Illinois, up by 29.5 percent (Cotton, 2012).

Politicians and members of the public have been asking why the costs of running colleges and universities are so high. One popular answer has been that much of the expense is due to excessive increases in faculty salaries. However, according to a 2012 survey of 1,251 American higher education institutions sponsored by the American Association of University Professors,

Full-time faculty salaries . . . on average, rose 1.8 percent in the 2011–12 academic year, an increase that was swallowed up by a 3 percent inflation rate. When adjusted for inflation, faculty salaries fell by an average of 1.2 percent. Over the past three decades tuition has increased at a much faster rate than full-time faculty salaries. . . . The contrast is starkest at public institutions, where tuition and fees have increased over the past decade by 72 percent when accounting for inflation, largely in response to declines in state support. During that same time, the salaries of public-college professors, when adjusted for inflation, rose by less than 1 percent at doctoral and baccalaureate institutions and fell by more than 5 percent at master's universities. (June, 2012, para. 4-5)

According to data from that same AAUP report, nationwide, the average 2012 annual faculty salaries by rank were: (a) full professor $113,176, (b) associate professor $78,565, (c) assistant professor $66,564, (d) instructor $47,847 (June, 2012). In contrast to the trends for faculty incomes, "Between 2006–2007 and 2010–2011, median [college] presidential salaries jumped by 9.8 percent, when adjusted for inflation, while median full-time faculty salaries rose by less than 2 percent" (June, 2012, para. 7).

Whereas salaries have accounted for some of the rise in college costs, many increases are due to higher equipment and facilities' maintenance expenses.

KINDS OF INSTITUTIONS

American higher education institutions have evolved into their present condition from various beginnings. Consider, for example, the following three types of development.

As noted in chapter 2, some present-day public universities began humbly as a year or two of post-high-school classes designed to train elementary school teachers or artisans in a trade. The classes were next separated from the high school to form a "normal school" or "technical school" that would, over the years, morph into a four-year college which added liberal arts that were not intended to be "mere vocational training." As a next step, graduate studies developed and led to a master's degree. More specialized fields of learning were gradually adopted, and the college expanded into a university composed of constituent schools or colleges (medicine, engineering, law, education, architecture, and the like). Doctoral studies were added—PhD, MD, LLD, DDS, EdD. Such, then, is one frequent pattern of development of present-day universities.

Another pattern by which hundreds of the nation's private institutions evolved consisted of a religious denomination founding a college whose purpose was to prepare clergy and to educate youths in the denomination's worldview. The two earliest higher learning institutions in the United States—Harvard and Yale—were created for such a purpose.

A third pattern began with the congressional Morrill Act of 1862/1890, which granted federal land in each state for the founding of an agriculture-and-mechanical college. Over the decades, those colleges have expanded into university-style institutions and, in most cases, their titles have been changed from A&M College to State University.

As illustrated by these three patterns of growth, over the decades American higher education institutions have become larger and more complex. The people who influence the nature of a college (legislators, members of governing boards, college administrators, faculty members, alumni) have not been content with the original form of their institution and thus have pressed for growth. Part of their effort has been motivated by a desire to enhance their school's prestige—its reputation locally, nationally, and internationally. That reputation is most often reflected in (a) the activities of prestigious graduates, (b) the amount and quality of attention the institution receives in the public press, (c) the fame of faculty members that derives from their publications, performances, and products, and (d) successful grant-seeking, technological innovation, and entrepreneurial skills of faculty members. The latter—grants and entrepreneurial and technological innovation—is likely to be valued highly in economic and political climates characterized by decreases in funding for higher education. The chance of gaining fame is greatest in colleges and universities that provide faculty members with the time, facilities, and encouragement (pressure) to do research and publish the results. To provide that time, faculty members are given light teaching loads or, in some cases, no teaching duties at all. Furthermore, professors who gain fame attract the highest salaries and the best job offers from other institutions.

In summary, we propose that the trend of higher education institutions to evolve from the teaching-only model toward the strong-research-and-light-teaching-load model will continue in the years ahead. However, there still are many colleges in which teaching is highly valued, so quality instruction will continue to be the chief focus of those schools' efforts. Such appears to be true of many four-year liberal arts colleges, technical institutes, and community colleges.

We also estimate that the number of two-year community colleges will increase substantially as a result of (a) crowding in four-year institutions and (b) the rapidly growing cost of a college education. As stringent financial limits have restricted the expansion of four-year schools, students have faced stiff competition in finding a place in those institutions. One way to accommodate the growing numbers consists of four-year schools giving priority to upper-division applicants, that is, to ones who enter in their junior year as transfers from junior colleges. This means that more students who pursue a bachelor's degree will need to complete their freshman and sophomore years in community colleges. Doing so reduces a student's college costs because tuition fees are substantially lower in junior colleges and the student can often live at home.

On the international scene, the recent growth of for-profit universities in rapidly developing economies (China, India, Malaysia, Brazil) will likely accelerate in the years ahead. These for-profit enterprises, funded chiefly by tuition fees,

> are the best way for emerging markets to build a skilled labor force, create more jobs, broaden the consumer base, and ultimately sustain economic growth. At the same time, for-profit higher education creates massive opportunities for investors that have only just begun to be realized. . . . In India, for example, single campuses have revenues as

high as $150 million with 50 percent profit margins and 35 percent internal rates of return. In Malaysia private higher education is a market worth $2.4 billion. (Khanna and Khemka, 2012, p. 62)

Thus the financial potential of for-profits outside the United States is lauded. In contrast, in the United States for-profit institutions, while profitable for shareholders have come under heavy criticism for targeting lower income and minority students who incur enormous debt as they pursue degrees that that do not result in kinds of employment that were promised (Taylor and Appel, 2014).

KINDS OF JOBS

In chapter 3 we traced recent trends in the types of positions available in higher education. Those trends feature

- A reduction in the proportion of faculty members in academic-ladder jobs that entitled them to fringe benefits (medical, dental, certain privileges), voting rights in department decisions, sabbatical leaves, and a pension upon retirement.
- A dramatic increase in part-time and temporary appointments that carry no fringe benefits, voting rights, sabbatical leaves, or pensions. This includes part-time online teaching appointments.
- The extensive use of graduate student assistants for teaching and for help with research-and-development projects.

We expect that these trends will not only continue into the future but will increase, particularly as a result of diminishing funds to support higher education and with growing numbers of students pressing for admission to college. As a consequence, more people who choose a career in college teaching will be part-timers, often obliged to teach several classes simultaneously in more than one institution or to hold another job in another occupation (office worker, computer programmer, writer, personal tutor) while teaching a class or two, perhaps in the evening.

METHODS OF INSTRUCTION

Dramatic technological advances over the past three decades have conspired with stringent economic conditions to alter ways professors are able to teach. We imagine that the years ahead will witness

The expansion of online classes available to students. Not only can online classes serve large numbers of students at a distance, but they don't require the expensive physical facilities of traditional colleges. However, online classes cannot substitute adequately for laboratories that students need to gain hands-on skill in the sciences, engineering, teaching, and physical education.

Even further expansions in classroom uses of technologies for teaching and learning. Ubiquitous student use of electronic notebooks, and smart phones for accessing course websites, submitting written assignments, searching for information, reading textbooks, and conferring with classmates and instructors.

As a result, you are likely to increase your marketability by developing your teaching-related technological skills, particular if you aim for a faculty position in a teaching institution. Having online teaching experience in many instances would be an advantage, as well.

IMPLICATIONS FOR PROSPECTIVE PROFESSORS

The following suggestions for individuals who are considering a career in higher education are based not only on the contents of this chapter but on the previous chapters of this book as well. We believe that you could profit from:

Reviewing the types of institutions described in chapter 2, then selecting the three types that you believe are best suited to (a) your academic preparation, (b) your desired working environment, (c) the kinds of students you wish to work with, (d) the sorts of activities you would be expected to conduct (teaching, research, performance, product creation), and (e) the geographic location in which you would like to live. Then identify which of your three types of institutions you chose is your first preference, second preference, and third preference.

Reviewing the types of jobs described in chapter 3, then selecting several types that you find most appealing in terms of the kind of appointment you would prefer. The phrase *kind of appointment* refers to both the title you would bear and the kinds of activities your job would involve. Examples of titles are full-time assistant professor, part-time adjunct professor, interim instructor, teaching fellow, and research professor. Examples of kinds of activities are full-time classroom teaching, classroom teaching plus research, teaching and counseling, classroom teaching and thesis advising, and full-time teaching online

With your preferred types of institutions and jobs in hand, you are prepared to survey hundreds of currently available job openings by entering the descriptor *college teaching positions* and your content area into an Internet search or by visiting websites that have repositories of higher education position listings, such as the *Chronicle of Higher Education*. You may also wish to ask for the job hunting help that can be provided by the job placement bureau of the university you have attended, and register for job announcements and position advertisements through the professional organizations affiliated with your discipline.

CONCLUSION

The dual purpose of this chapter has been (a) to estimate what the condition of higher education will likely be in years to come and (b) to suggest how individuals who are considering a career in college teaching may profit from understanding those conditions as they plan their future.

References

AAUP (American Association of University Professors). (1940). *1940 Statement of principles on academic freedom and tenure.* Retrieved from www.aaup.org/report/1940-statement-principles-academic-freedom-and-tenure.

——. (1990a). *On preventing conflicts of interest in government-sponsored research at universities.* Retrieved from www.aaup.org/report/preventing-conflicts-interest-government-sponsored-research-universities.

——. (1990b). *Sexual harassment: Suggested policy and procedure for handling complaints.* Retrieved from www.aaup.org/AAUP/pubsres/policydocs/contents/sexharass.htm.

——. (1990c). *Statement on plagiarism.* Retrieved from www.aaup.org/report/statement-plagiarism.

——. (2004). *On professors assigning their own texts to students.* Retrieved from www.aaup.org/report/professors-assigning-their-own-texts-students.

——. (2009). *Statement on professional ethics.* Retrieved from www.aaup.org/report/statement-professional-ethics.

——. (2013). *Statement on conflicts of interest.* (Original statement published 1990). Retrieved from www.aaup.org/report/statement-conflicts-interest.

Academic Senate for California Community Colleges. (2010). *Community college reform act: Part I: Responsibilities.* Retrieved from www.asccc.org/communities/local-senates/handbook/partI.

African Studies Association. (2014). *African Studies Association membership services and pre-meeting registration.* Retrieved from journals.cambridge.org/action/memServ Home?name=ASAHome.

American Classical League. (2014). *Become a member.* Retrieved from www.aclclassics. org/pages/membership.

American Educational Research Association. (2013). *Membership categories.* Retrieved from www.aera.net/Membership/MembershipCategories/tabid/10229/Default.aspx.

American Federation of Teachers—AFL-CIO. (2014). *A union of professionals.* Retrieved from www.aft.org/about/.

American Psychological Association. (2014). *How to join APA.* Retrieved from www. apa.org/about/students.aspx.

American Public Health Association. (2014). *Poster session guidelines.* APHA meetings. Retrieved from www.apha.org/meetings/sessions/PosterSessionGuidelines.htm.

American Society for Biochemistry and Molecular Biology (2014). *ASBMB member types.* Retrieved from www.asbmb.org/Page.aspx?id=56.

American Sociological Association (n.d.). *What are sections?* Retrieved from www. asanet.org/sections/definition.cfm.

Boise State University. (2013). *Faculty promotion guidelines.* Retrieved from policy. boisestate.edu/academic-affairs-faculty-administration/policy-title-faculty-promotion-guidelines/.

Boston University. (2007). *Classification of ranks and titles.* Retrieved from www.bu.edu/handbook/appointments-and-promotions/classification-of-ranks-and-titles/.

Bradley, G. (2004). Contingent faculty and the new academic labor system. *Academe Online.* Retrieved from www.aaup.org/AAUP/pubsres/academe/2004/JF/Feat/brad.htm.

Brandeis University. (2014). *Brandeis: Fast facts.* Retrieved from www.brandeis.edu/about/facts/index.html.

Caltech. (2013). *At a glance.* Retrieved from www.caltech.edu/at-a-glance.

Canfield, D. D. (2011). Review of *Barn Dances* (Albany Records TROY 1234), *Fanfare Magazine, 34,* (May/June), 159–60.

Casper, G. (1996). *Letter to James Fellows.* Retrieved from www.stanford.edu/dept/pres-provost/president/speeches/961206gcfallow.html/

Censky, A. (2011, June 13). Surging college costs price out middle class. *CNN Money.* Retrieved from money.cnn.com/2011/06/13/news/economy/college_tuition_middle_class/.

Cornell University Libraries. (2013). *Book reviews—A finding guide.* Retrieved from guides.library.cornell.edu/bookreviews.

Cotton, A. (2012, April 13). CU president: State funding for colleges imperiled. *Denver Post.* Retrieved from www.denverpost.com/reakingnews/ci_20390751/cu-president-state-funding-colleges-imperiled?source=rss.

Davidson, C. (2008, June 6). *Should digital scholarship "count" towards tenure?* Retrieved from www.hastac.org/blogs/cathy-davidson/should-digital-scholarship-count-to wards-tenure.

———. (2010, June 6). *Should blogs count for tenure and promotion?* Retrieved from www.hastac.org/blogs/cathy-davidson/should-blogs-count-tenure-and-promotion.

Duke University. (n.d.). *Provost's Office of Faculty Affairs: Criteria for tenure.* Retrieved from www.facultyaffairs.provost.duke.edu/criteria.html.

Eastern Oklahoma State University. (2014). *Student and campus life, Placement office.* Retrieved from www.eosc.edu/departments/placement.html.

Edvisors. (2013). CollegeToolKit.com. Anthropology and Archeology Teachers, post-secondary: Nature of the work. Retrieved from www.collegetoolkit.com/careers/anthropology_and_archeology_teachers__postsecondary/tasks/25-1061.00.aspx.

Evelyn, J. (2005, October 28). Views and characteristics of community college professors. *Chronicle of Higher Education, 28,* B10.

Fiske, E. (2014). *Fiske guide to colleges.* Naperville, IL: Sourcebooks.

Fulbright. (2012). *Fulbright program.* Retrieved from eca.state.gov/files/bureau/fulbright_program_one-pager.pdf.

Furgason, R. (November 19, 2007) How the university tenure system works. *Caller.com.* Retrieved from www.caller.com/news/2007/nov/19/how-the-university-tenure-system-works/.

Hanselman, K. (2012, April 19). Interview conducted by Marie Iding in Honolulu, Hawaii.

Harvard University. (2011). *Tenure/ladder attribute fact sheet.* Retrieved from vpf-web.harvard.edu/training/enews/html/201005a-attachments/Tenure-Ladder%20Attribute%20Factsheet.pdf.

———. (2014). *History of Harvard University.* Retrieved from www.harvard.edu/history.

Hoeller, K. (2007, November 13). The future of the contingent faculty movement. *Inside Higher Ed.* Retrieved from www.insidehighered.com/views/2007/11/13/hoeller.

Hunter College. (2013). *Distinguished lecturer—Chemistry. Faculty positions.* Retrieved from hr.hunter.cuny.edu/jobs/facultyjobs.html#8543.

Iding, M. and Thomas, R. M. (in press). *A guide to teaching at colleges and universities.*

Jaschik, S. (2008, April 14). Faculty salaries and priorities. *Inside Higher Ed.* Retrieved from www.insidehighered.com/news/2008/04/14/aaup.

Jenkins, R. (2003, November 14). Not a bad gig. *Chronicle of Higher Education, 50* (12), C1-C2.

Juilliard School. (2013). *Juilliard's mission.* Retrieved from www.juilliard.edu/about/juilliards-mission.

June, A. W. (2012, April 8). Professors seek to reframe salary debate. *Chronicle of Higher Education.* Retrieved from chronicle.com/article/faculty-salaries-barely-budge-2012/131432.

Katsinas, S. G., Buchholz, D. A., Priest, B. J., Palmer , J. C., and Tollefson, T. A. (2004, October 26*). State funding for community colleges: Perceptions from the field.* Retrieved fromwww.statedirectors.org/surveys/StateFIN.pdf.

Khanna, P., and Khemka, K. (2012, January–February). Enroll the world in for-profit universities. *Harvard Business Review,* Issue 1, p. 62.

Kolata, G. (2013, April 8). Scientific articles accepted (personal checks, too). *New York Times.* Retrieved from www.nytimes.com/2013/04/08/health/for-scientists-an-exploding-world-of-pseudo-academia.html?pagewanted=all&_r=0.

Marion Military Institute. (2013). *Mission statement.* Retrieved from www.marionmilitary.edu/about/history.cms.

Michigan State University. (n.d.). *Computer science TA handbook.* Retrieved from www.cs.umd.edu/grad/ta-handbook.

National Center for Education Statistics. (2012). *Tuition costs of colleges and universities. Institute of Education Sciences: Fast facts.* Retrieved from nces.ed.gov/fastfacts/display.asp?id=76.

National Education Association. (2014). *About NEA.* Retrieved from www.nea.org/home/2580.htm.

National Science Foundation. (2005, July). Chapter V–Grantee standards: 510 Conflict-of-interest policies. *NSF publication No. 05-13.* Retrieved from www.nsf.gov/pubs/manuals/gpm05_131/gpm5.jsp#510.

New York Univeristy Steinhardt. (2014). *Sabbatical leave.* Retrieved from steinhardt.nyu.edu/faculty_affairs/sabbatical_leave.

Northeastern University. (2013). *Human resources management: Lecturer.* Retrieved from neu.peopleadmin.com/postings/23887.

Northern Arizona University. (2013). *Human Capital Management: Lecturer.* Retrieved from hr.peoplesoft.nau.edu/psp/ph90prta/EMPLOYEE/HCM/c/HRS_HRAM.HRS_CE.GBL?Page=HRS_CE_JOB_DTL&Action=A&JobOpeningId=600664&SiteId=2&PostingSeq=1.

Northwestern University School of Law. (2013). *Promotion: Appointment and promotion policies. Clinical faculty (Bluhm Legal Clinic).* Retrieved from www.law.northwestern.edu/research-faculty/faculty/policies/promotion/.

Odland, S. (2012, March 24). College costs out of control. *Forbes.* Retrieved from www.forbes.com/sites/steveodland/2012/03/24/college-costs-are-soaring/.

Ohio State University College of Engineering. (2014). *Nepotism policy.* Retrieved from engineering.osu.edu/hr/nepotism-policy.

Oklahoma State University. (2013). *Mission statement.* Retrieved from system.okstate.edu/.

Pasadena City College. (2007). *Pasadena area community college district: Official academic salary schedule.* Retrieved from www.pasadena.edu/hr/documents/0708A.pdf.

Princeton Review. (2014). *The Best 378 Colleges.* Princeton, NJ: Princeton Review.

Pritchard, J. (2009, March). Review of American Reflections. *The Flute Network.* Retrieved from www.flutenet.com/mar09rec.htm.

Reed College Admission. (2014). *College rankings.* Retrieved from web.reed.edu/apply/news_and_articles/college_rankings.html.

The Rodda Project. (2007, August 14). *The Back Bench.* Retrieved from thebackbench. blogspot.com/2007/08/collective-bargaining-in-california.html.

Stanford University News Service. (1997, February 18). *Push to increase percentage of faculty salaries covered by endowment.* Retrieved from news.stanford.edu/pr/97/970218endowed.html.

Stanford University. (2014). *Stanford University common data set 2013–2014: Enrollment and persistence.* Retrieved from ucomm.stanford.edu/cds/2013.html#enrollment.

Stanford University Libraries (2014). *Copyright & fair use overview.* Retrieved from fairuse.stanford.edu/.

State University of New York at Brockport. (2011). *Guidelines for personnel decisions: Department of Chemistry: Weighting of activities and accomplishments in teaching, scholarship, and service.* Retrieved from www.brockport.edu/chemistry/admin/apt.htm.

Taylor, A., and Appel, H. (2014, September 23). Subprime students: How for-profit universities make a killing by exploiting college dreams. *Mother Jones.* Retrieved from www.motherjones.com/politics/2014/09/for-profit-university-subprime-student-poor-minority.

Tennessee Board of Regents. (2008). *Faculty promotion at universities: Policy/guideline: Academic ranks.* Retrieved from policies.tbr.edu/policies/faculty-promotion-uni versities.

Tufts University. (2014). *Tufts at a glance.* Retrieved from www.tufts.edu/home/get_to_know_tufts/.

University of California, Berkeley (2009). *Table 17-1: Non-senate instructional (NSI) Unit 18 Academic Standard Table of Pay Rates, Minimum Scale 10/1/11.* Retrieved from www.ucop.edu/academic-personnel/_files/1112/table17-1_17-2.pdf.

———. (2013). *Total enrollment.* Retrieved from opa.berkeley.edu/institutionaldata/campusenroll.htm.

University of California, Irvine. (2011). *UCI chairs and professorships.* Retrieved from www.ap.uci.edu/distinctions/endowed.html.

University of California, Los Angeles. (2011). *Endowed chair holders.* Retrieved from www.apo.ucla.edu/academiclistings_chairholders.html#a.

University of California—Office of the President. (2005). *Appointment and promotion—Health sciences clinical professor series.* Retrieved from www.ucop.edu/academic-personnel/_files/apm/apm-278.pdf.

University of California, San Diego. (2011). *Endowed chairs: Frequently asked questions.* Retrieved from dah.ucsd.edu/giving/Endowed%20Chairs%20FAQs.pdf.

University of California, Santa Barbara. (2011). *Endowed chairs.* Retrieved from www.ia.ucsb.edu/dev/endow.shtml.

University of Maryland Baltimore County. (2002). *Clinical professor promotion criteria.* Retrieved from userpages.umbc.edu/~blunck/pdf/1.%20TEACHING/5.%20UMBC%20CLINICAL%20PROMOTION%20CRITERIA/Clinical%20Professor%20Promotion%20Criteria.pdf.

University of Maryland Libraries. (2011). *Primary, secondary, tertiary sources.* Retrieved from www.lib.umd.edu/tl/guides/primary-sources.

University of Michigan. (1992.) *Mission and vision statements.* Retrieved from www.provost.umich.edu/reports/slfstudy/ir/criteria/.

University of Northern Colorado. (2013). *A short history of UNC.* Retrieved from www.unco.edu/pres/sh.htm.

University of North Texas, Political Science Department (n.d.). *Criteria for tenure with promotion to associate professor.* Retrieved from www.vpaa.unt.edu/files/Faculty/ChairsCouncil/PSCIPATPolicy.doc.

University of Rochester. (2009). *Proposal for a clinical faculty track (Draft).* Retrieved from schwert.ssb.rochester.edu/clinical0903.pdf.

University of Texas Southwestern Medical Center. (2011). *Information about faculty appointments, promotion, tenure, evaluation and non-reappointment.* Retrieved from www.austingme.com/templates/GraduateMedicalEducation/Assets/information_about_faculty_appointments_promotion_tenure_evaluation_and_non-reappointment.pdf.

USC Dornsife, College of Letters, Arts, and Sciences (2014). *Your college teaching assistantship: Teaching assistant responsibilities.* Retrieved from dornsife.usc.edu/your-college-teaching-assistantship/.

U.S. Department of Education. (2013). *Accreditation in the United States.* Retrieved from www2.ed.gov/admins/finaid/accred/accreditation.html#Overview.

U.S. News Staff. (2014a). Education—Colleges. *USNews.* Retrieved from colleges.usnews.rankingsandreviews.com/best-colleges.

———. (2014b). *Grad school compass.* Retrieved from grad-schools.usnews.rankingsandreviews.com/best-graduate-schools.

Washington State University. (2009). *What is a land-grant college?* Retrieved from http://ext.wsu.edu/documents/landgrant.pdf.

Whitman College. (2013). *Professorships and chairs.* Retrieved from www.whitman.edu/giving/ways-of-giving/endowments.

Wikipedia (n.d.). Tenure. Retrieved from en.wikipedia.org/wiki/Tenure, para 3.

WIPO. (n.d. a) World Intellectual Property Organization. *Guidelines on developing intellectual property policy for universities and R&D organizations.* Retrieved from www.wipo.int/export/sites/www/uipc/en/guidelines/pdf/ip_policy.pdf.

———. (n.d. b) World Intellectual Property Organization. *What is intellectual property?* Retrieved from www.wipo.int/export/sites/www/freepublications/en/intproperty/450/wipo_pub_450.pdf.

Yale University. (2013). *About Yale.* Retrieved from www.yale.edu/about/mission.html.

About the Authors

Marie Iding (PhD, University of California, Santa Barbara) is a professor of educational psychology at the University of Hawai'i at Mānoa, where she has taught for over twenty years. She has also taught, and presented research or workshops in diverse locations around the world, including American Samoa, Chuuk (Federated States of Micronesia), Vietnam, Germany, Switzerland, South Africa, Kenya, Spain, Portugal, Fiji, Australia, Jamaica, Poland, and Scotland.

R. Murray Thomas (PhD, Stanford University) is professor emeritus of educational psychology at the University of California, Santa Barbara, where he also directed the program in international education. His list of professional publications exceeds four hundred, including fifty-nine books for which he served as author, coauthor, or editor.